BORDER BATTLES

BORDER BATTLES

NORTHUMBERLAND IN THE ANGLO-SCOTTISH WARS, 1018–1513

CHRIS PEERS

Pen & Sword
MILITARY
AN IMPRINT OF PEN & SWORD BOOKS LTD.
YORKSHIRE – PHILADELPHIA

First published in Great Britain in 2025 by
PEN AND SWORD MILITARY
An imprint of
Pen & Sword Books Limited
Yorkshire – Philadelphia

ISBN 978 1 39903 971 0

A CIP catalogue record for this book is available from the British Library.

Typeset in Times New Roman 12/16 by
SJmagic DESIGN SERVICES, India.
Printed and bound in the UK by CPI Group (UK) Ltd.

The Publisher's authorised representative in the EU for product safety is Authorised Rep Compliance Ltd., Ground Floor, 71 Lower Baggot Street, Dublin D02 P593, Ireland.
www.arccompliance.com

For a complete list of Pen & Sword titles please contact
PEN & SWORD BOOKS LIMITED
George House, Units 12 & 13, Beevor Street, Off Pontefract Road,
Barnsley, South Yorkshire, S71 1HN, England
E-mail: enquiries@pen-and-sword.co.uk
Website: www.pen-and-sword.co.uk

or

PEN AND SWORD BOOKS
1950 Lawrence Rd, Havertown, PA 19083, USA
E-mail: uspen-and-sword@casematepublishers.com
Website: www.penandswordbooks.com

MIX
Paper | Supporting responsible forestry
FSC® C013604

Contents

Acknowledgements

IN THE COURSE of my research in the late spring of 2023, I traversed all of the battlefields featured in this book, but my visits to two of them – at Otterburn and Flodden – coincided with weather so typically Northumbrian that I could obtain no useable photographs. Special thanks are therefore due to Geoffrey Carter of the Revitalising Redesdale Project for providing the pictures of the Otterburn battlefield, and to my daughter, Megan, for her photographs of Flodden.

Introduction

'Heroes Killed, and Armies Routed'

THIS BOOK WAS conceived as a complementary volume to my previous two books on medieval British battles – *The Highland Battles* (2020) and *Clan Battles* (2023), both published by Pen & Sword – which discussed the warfare of the period in the light of my visits to some of the lesser-known battlefields of northern and western Scotland. Northumberland, like the Highlands and Islands of Scotland, is one of my favourite places, and any excuse to wander around its quiet backwaters is always welcome. However, in the present case the experience of writing about it has inevitably been rather different. The first two books focused mainly on relatively little-known, small-scale encounters which took place in some of the most remote and sparsely populated corners of the British Isles. Few of the battlefields are commemorated on the ground, and in some cases their exact locations are still unknown or controversial. Northumberland, the most northerly county in England, is by the standards of that overcrowded country relatively empty and undeveloped, but it is nevertheless home to many more people than its Scottish equivalents. The Northumberland County Council website (northumberland.gov.uk) gives a figure of 163 inhabitants per square mile, which converts to about sixty-three to the square kilometre. In Caithness and Sutherland, the two Scottish counties which feature most prominently in the other two books, the equivalent figure per square kilometre is five (Highlands and Islands Enterprise, at hie.co.uk). Furthermore Northumberland is much closer to larger centres of population which lie outside its borders, the nearest of which are Tyneside and Edinburgh, so here there has been more development, more tourism and more archaeological research. Instead of struggling to identify features in the landscape which might indicate where a specific battle was fought, the visitor will almost always find a monument of some sort, and more often than not a marked battlefield trail, complete with interpretation boards. But this does not necessarily mean that there is nothing new to say about these places or the events which took place there. I have attempted to put each battle into its wider context, giving a brief account of the political background, concentrating more closely on the evolution of the equipment and tactics which were in use at the relevant period. But perhaps equally important is the terrain over which the battles were fought, and visiting and walking over each site has given me some interesting insights into how geography and military systems interacted with each other. Sometimes these have confirmed in my mind the validity of previous writers' conclusions, while on other occasions they have led me to question them, but in all cases any errors or misinterpretations are mine alone. I have included brief notes at the end of each chapter which may help any interested readers who wish to investigate the sites for themselves and reach their own conclusions.

Daniel Defoe, writing in the 1720s, thought of Northumberland as one great battlefield, observing that 'Every place shews you ruin'd castles, Roman altars, inscriptions, monuments of battles, of heroes killed, and armies routed' (*A Tour Through the Whole Island of Great Britain*, 1724–27, quoted in Groom, 2022). His impression can be confirmed by a glance at any modern map showing recognized battlefield sites in England, such as those produced by the Battlefields Trust. There is a cluster of such locations in Yorkshire, another cluster further north, along the border with Scotland, and joining them together a string of sites roughly following the line of the Great North Road, now the A1, which connects London with Edinburgh. This phenomenon is due principally to geography. The northern part of the main 'Island of Great Britain' is divided between two kingdoms, England and Scotland, and the border between them runs from one coast to the other, roughly from north-east to south-west. South of the border, in northern England, the rugged Pennine hills run from north to south down the middle of the island, forming a barrier which meant that if the two kingdoms were at war – which between the eleventh and sixteenth centuries AD was the case as often as not – the only feasible invasion routes lay along one coast or the other. For a number of reasons, the eastern route, through what is now Northumberland, was by far the most popular. The coastal strip is wider here than in the west and the climate somewhat drier, which made the going better for marching armies and supplies easier to find. The North Sea coast is less exposed to the prevailing winds than the Atlantic on the western side, and thanks to the long history of trade with Europe across the North Sea, most of the ports and safe harbours are also found there. So fleets – usually English ones – could operate more effectively in support of the land armies. But most importantly, the main centres of wealth and power in Scotland and northern England were to be found at either end of the eastern coastal corridor. When it was founded in the ninth century AD, the Scottish kingdom which replaced that of the earlier Picts was centred around Perth at the mouth of the River Tay. After its capital was established at Edinburgh a century or so later, its population and wealth continued to be concentrated along the east coast. In England, the great cathedral city of Durham was only 60 miles from the border, and a similar distance further south was York, the principal city of the north and one of the richest in the country. So it is not surprising that almost every major invasion of one kingdom by the other went through Northumberland, and that even raiders with more limited objectives, such as stealing cattle or other booty, found it the nearest and most lucrative target.

In the medieval period, the north of England as a whole was the poorest and least densely populated part of the realm, a situation which did not change until the Industrial Revolution. Barrow (1992) points out that the 'fifteenth' duty on imports and exports which the Crown earned from the three major northern ports – Hull, York and Newcastle – combined, added up to less than that paid by Southampton alone. Professor Barrow also paints a vivid picture of a primitive northern English landscape in which the ubiquitous stone houses and walls of today were absent, the countryside was open and unenclosed, and the villages and even the churches were usually built of wood. Crops such as oats and barley were grown wherever possible, but the herding of livestock played a much more prominent part in the economy than further south, where the warmer climate and richer soils made arable farming more productive. Barrow quotes the twelfth-century writer Reginald of Durham's *Miracles of Saint Cuthbert*, in which the story is told of a poor farmer who was forced to flee to Scotland to escape from a tyrannical landlord. His herds of cattle, sheep and horses made such a noise on the road that they threatened to betray him to pursuers, until Cuthbert miraculously made his oppressors deaf. The fourteenth-century chronicler Jean Froissart echoes this with his description of Northumberland as 'a wild country full of deserts and mountains, and very poor in everything except cattle' (Jolliffe, 1967). This abundance of livestock is worth noting because it seems to be a rule that the presence of large numbers of cattle especially, in a frontier district like this one, was an irresistible temptation to lawlessness. Cattle are capable of travelling long distances at speed and of fording rivers at which other animals would baulk, and being herd animals by nature they are fairly easy to drive en masse. They were also fundamental to the economy of many of the Scottish communities north of the Tweed, so – political considerations aside – it is not surprising that an industry should grow up around cattle rustling. Of course the English were just as often perpetrators as victims, and few accounts of military campaigns in our period are complete without a tally of the animals stolen and driven across the border in one direction or the other.

Before going any further, it is necessary to draw a distinction between the late medieval and modern county of Northumberland and the ancient kingdom, and later earldom, of Northumbria. In the seventh and eighth centuries AD, England was not a united country, the Anglo-Saxon-speaking area which roughly corresponds to its modern borders being divided among seven main kingdoms, an arrangement which later became known as the Heptarchy. In the late seventh century, the whole region east of the Pennine hills, between the River Humber in the south and the Firth of Forth in the north, was part of the Kingdom of Northumbria ('north of the Humber'), which had been established in the 650s by the amalgamation of the two earlier kingdoms of Deira and Bernicia. Northumberland as we know it today covers a much smaller area, roughly between the rivers Tyne in the south and Tweed in the north; it thus excludes all the territory between the Tweed and the Firth of Forth, which is now part of Scotland, as well as the English counties of Durham and Yorkshire. This is the region which is the main subject of this book. It is bounded on the west by the watershed of the Pennines and on the east by the North Sea. The western half of the county is mostly moorland and hill pasture, unsuitable for arable farming because of the altitude and poor soils, but between the hills and the sea is a wide stretch of relatively flat land, whose heavy clay soil has been farmed for thousands of years. This contrasts with the opposite coast of England, in the west, where the hills are steeper and extend much closer to the sea, and with the sandstone soils of the gently undulating land north of the Tweed known as the Merse, now part of Scotland, which despite its more northerly latitude has always been regarded as more productive (Pease, 1912). As well as the Tyne and Tweed, several other rivers flow from west to east across the Northumberland coastal plain to the sea; the main ones are, from south to north, the Blyth, Wansbeck, Coquet and Aln; further north still, the River Till rises in the hills and flows northward, roughly parallel to the coast, to meet the Tweed. None of these intervening streams is easily navigable, however, and none has ever presented a serious obstacle to the movement of armies.

Until recently, most scholars, relying on the account of the Northumbrian monk Bede, whose *Ecclesiastical History of the English People* (Sherley-Price, 1955) was completed in the 730s, have supposed that both Bernicia and Deira were founded by the Angles, a Germanic people who – together with the Saxons – had migrated from the continent of Europe in the fifth century and displaced the native Britons. Modern research tends to play down the extent of these migrations, and it is very unlikely that the Britons were slaughtered en masse, as Bede implies (see my *Offa and the Mercian Wars*, Chapter 2, for a discussion of this issue), but there were certainly cultural differences between the Northumbrians and their neighbours. Unlike the people of Cumbria on the other side of the Pennines, for example, they retained very few traces of an earlier Celtic language. Barrow cites several examples of surviving Celtic personal names, principally in the western part of the county bordering on Cumbria, as late as the thirteenth century, but the Gaelic tongue which was spreading through Scotland from the west in the early Middle Ages made no progress south of the Forth. The place names of the northern part of the Northumbrian kingdom – the former Bernicia, roughly corresponding to south-eastern Scotland and the modern county of Northumberland – are overwhelmingly English. Further south, in modern Yorkshire, they have been overlaid by a strong Danish element traceable to the ninth-century Viking invasions, but the wide plain of Northumberland, though open to the North Sea and well supplied with landing beaches, seems never to have appealed to the invaders. One reason might have been the lack of wide, gently flowing rivers which could provide easy access to the interior; another possible factor was that the heavy soils of Northumberland were less suitable for the newcomers' farming techniques. It has been observed that in Lincolnshire, the Danes tended to settle on the lighter, sandy soils on the ridges (Wood, 1986), whereas in the north, the high ground is usually a long way from the sea, and too high and infertile to be suitable for any form of arable farming. It is also possible that the plain, which had been the centre of English power in the north for at least three centuries, was already too densely settled, and the native population too well versed in warfare from its long history of conflicts with the Picts and Scots, for it to be easily displaced.

In the eighth century, Northumbria was one of the great centres of English learning and culture, based around the monasteries at Lindisfarne and Jarrow, but the long and accessible coastline made it very vulnerable when Viking fleets from Scandinavia began to navigate the North Sea in the last decades of the century. The first recorded Viking attack in the region took place in 793 at the Abbey of Lindisfarne, on the island of that name – also known as Holy Island – near the present-day village of Bamburgh, which was then the seat of the secular rulers of northern Northumbria. But although the coast, and in particular its wealthy religious sites, were frequently raided, the invaders did not attempt to push directly inland. Instead, when the Danish Great Army captured York in 867, they seized territory further south in the region between the rivers Tees and Humber, which had formed part of the former Deira and latterly of modern Yorkshire. This area remained under occupation for most of the next ninety years, first by the Danes and later by Dublin Vikings of Norwegian origin. Meanwhile, further north, a tenuously unified Kingdom of Scotland was coming into being, but the boundary between it and the Northumbrians was by no means firmly established, especially as a dialect of the English language was still spoken as far north as Edinburgh, a town which may still have been a Northumbrian outpost until as late as 950. It has been convincingly argued that the event which made permanent the division of the north of Britain into two warring kingdoms, and thus set the tone of Anglo-Scottish relations for the remainder of the medieval period, took place far from the border country, in an unknown location and on an unknown day in the year 937 (Livingston, 2021).

Athelstan and the Battle of Brunanburgh

During the reign of Alfred the Great (871–99), the Anglo-Saxon kingdoms of Wessex and Mercia in southern England had gradually turned the tide against the Danish invaders, who by then had overrun most of the north and east of the country. In the first quarter of the tenth century, Alfred's successors, the kings of Wessex, emerged as the rulers of an embryonic English nation. Finally, in 927,

Alfred's grandson, Athelstan, captured York, the last stronghold of the Danes in England, and soon afterwards he hosted a great gathering at Eamont near Penrith, at which he received the submission of the most eminent of the remaining independent rulers in Britain. Those who acknowledged his overlordship were Constantin II mac Aeda, the king of the Scots; Owain ap Dyfnwal of Strathclyde; Hywel ap Cadell, known as Hywel Dda or 'the Good', king of Deheubarth in South Wales; Owain, king of neighbouring Gwent; and Eadred of Bamburgh, the son of Eadwulf, who had until then been the ruler of an effectively independent Northumbria, cut off from the rest of England by the Danish occupation of York. According to the *Anglo-Saxon Chronicle* (Swanton, 2000), the participants at the meeting pledged to keep the peace and prohibit devil worship (by which was presumably meant the last vestiges of the pre-Christian religions of the island), and then parted amicably. From this time onwards, Athelstan and his successors are usually referred to as the rulers, not just of Wessex or of 'the Anglo-Saxons', but of the Kingdom of England.

Only six years later, however, the *Anglo-Saxon Chronicle* tells us that Athelstan launched an invasion of Scotland. Advancing by both land and sea, he ravaged much of the country, even though he failed to bring the Scots to battle. His motive is unknown, although the twelfth-century chronicler John of Worcester alleged that the Scots had already broken the agreement made at Eamont. Nevertheless, Constantin and his neighbours obviously considered that their independence was under threat, and in 937 they formed an alliance with the aim of removing Athelstan. In the autumn of that year, Olaf III Guthfrithson, the Norse King of Dublin, sailed to England with an army and joined forces with Constantin and Owain of Strathclyde. Athelstan marched north to meet them, and a great battle was fought at a place known as Brunanburgh. This seems to have been generally acknowledged as the biggest and bloodiest battle fought in England until then. Unfortunately our main source, an alliterative poem inserted into the *Anglo-Saxon Chronicle*, confines itself to a formulaic description of the fighting, with plenty of conventional images of shield walls and sword strokes, but no useful details of the location of the battle, the course of events or the tactics employed. It is generally supposed that the Battle of Vinheidi which features prominently in the Norse *Egil's Saga* refers to Brunanburgh, and the saga does provide a considerable amount of detail about the course of the fighting, but unfortunately its reliability is very doubtful (Oskarsdottir, 2004). For one thing, it names the Scottish king as one Olaf the Red, an error which presumably derives from confusion with Olaf Guthfrithson. It also goes on to tell of a confrontation between Athelstan and Erik Bloodaxe, who was a later ruler of York, even though in reality Athelstan died long before Erik even arrived in England. On the other hand, the fact that the battle is mentioned in an Icelandic saga, and that Athelstan has a prominent place in it, lends weight to the claim that there were Vikings fighting there on the English side. The eponymous hero, Egil Skallagrimson, is depicted not only as fighting for Athelstan but as spending much of his time in the royal presence, praising the king in his poetry and being richly rewarded in return.

It has recently been suggested in several media reports that the Brunanburgh battlefield has been definitively located at a site near Bromborough, on the Wirral peninsula on the west coast of England. A detailed examination of these claims is beyond the scope of this book, but they are based on excavations carried out by the organization Wirral Archaeology, which have revealed what appears to be a military camp of tenth-century date. See for example the Liverpool University Press blog for 2 October 2019: 'The Search for the Battle of Brunanburgh is Over'. There is an extensive literature about the location of this battle. Livingston (2021) is a very good recent discussion, although the conclusion which he reaches is at variance with that set out here. The find at Bromborough has been conflated with a long-debated but by no means definitely established identification of that town with the otherwise unknown place name Brunanburgh. Admittedly, the Wirral would be a logical landing place for a fleet coming across the

Irish Sea from Dublin, but to date no human remains or other finds have been reported which would prove that a battle took place on the Bromborough site. Furthermore, the claim needs to be considered in the light of the statement of John of Worcester, echoed in several other medieval sources, that the Dubliners arrived in England via the Humber estuary, on the east coast south of York. This suggests a site for the battle somewhere in the north-east of the country, which would have involved a longer sea voyage for Olaf's men but might have put them in a better position to link up with a Scottish army taking the traditional route into England, through Northumbria. *Egil's Saga* says that before meeting Athelstan at Brunanburgh, 'King Olaf' of Scotland had plundered Northumbria (by which he may have meant the whole of the former kingdom, including Yorkshire) and defeated an army led by the two earls who had been appointed by Athelstan to rule it. William of Malmesbury, another twelfth-century writer, says that Athelstan deliberately allowed the invaders to advance deep into English territory, and his contemporary Henry of Huntingdon adds that Olaf was joined by Danes living in England (Greenway, 1996). The latter statement might be evidence for a site in Yorkshire or Lincolnshire rather than further north in modern Northumberland, where as we have seen there appears never to have been a sizeable Danish immigrant population.

Egil's Saga says that Athelstan sent a formal challenge to his enemies and that they agreed to meet at a place called Wen Heath, where there was an expanse of moorland flat enough for the armies to deploy unhindered. The flanks were guarded by a forest on one side and a river on the other. The location was marked out in advance with hazel rods, in accordance with a traditional procedure for prearranged battles. According to this account there were two fights on successive days, in the first of which Aelfgir, one of the Northumbrian earls who had been defeated previously, lost again and fled the field, leaving the Vikings under Thorolf and Egil to save the day by attacking the enemy centre from the direction of the forest. On the following day, Thorolf rather recklessly tried the same manoeuvre again and led the

Vikings in another outflanking move along the edge of the forest, but this time he was ambushed by a Scottish detachment hidden in the trees and killed in the subsequent rout. Egil then rallied the troops, defeated the ambushers and charged into the flank of the Scottish main body in the centre. Seeing this, Athelstan brought up the Englishmen and won a great victory. In contrast to this dramatic (and possibly largely fictional) account, with its understandable emphasis on the Viking contribution to the victory, English sources tell us very little. From the *Anglo-Saxon Chronicle* we know only that Athelstan's West Saxons and their Mercian allies were victorious after a hard fight and the invaders eventually fled, leaving five kings and seven Norse jarls among the dead. The Irish *Annals of Clonmacnoise* claimed that the allied casualties totalled 34,800, and although this figure is both suspiciously precise and far too large for a medieval battle, the devastating losses among the enemies of the English do seem to have haunted their collective memory for the rest of the century. The *Anglo-Saxon Chronicle* concludes that 'Never yet in this island was there a greater slaughter of people felled by the sword's edges … since Angles and Saxons came here from the east', and continues with a grisly account of the wolves, eagles and ravens that gathered to feed on the corpses. Egil Skallagrimson's praise poem, quoted in *Egil's Saga*, echoes this image with its description of Athelstan as 'feeder of ravens', and goes on to claim that the victory had given him dominion over the whole of Britain: 'Even the Highland deer's paths [i.e. the northern parts of Scotland] belong to mighty Athelstan now.'

DRAWN AND ENGRAVED FOR LEWIS' TOPOGRAPHICAL DICTIONARY.

Chapter One

'Why Was I Spared to See These Times?' Carham, 1018

Date	c.1018
Location	In the vicinity of Carham on Tweed, Northumberland, west of Coldstream
Combatants	An allied army under King Malcolm II of Scotland and Owain of Strathclyde, versus local English forces under Uhtred son of Waltheof, Earl of Northumbria
Outcome	Scottish/Strathclyde victory

THE SPECTACULAR VICTORY at Brunanburgh may have saved central and southern England from invasion, but – the boasts of *Egil's Saga* notwithstanding – it did not lead to the English conquest of Scotland, nor did it bring lasting peace to the North. Athelstan died in 939, Olaf Guthfrithson taking advantage of the inexperience of his successor, Edmund, to take back York. The city remained in Norse hands as the capital of a revived Kingdom of York until 954, when the English King Eadred expelled Olaf's successor, Erik Bloodaxe, but it is unlikely that the kingdom's boundaries extended north of the River Tees, which today separates the counties of North Yorkshire and Durham. Between the Tees and Tyne rivers, in what is now County Durham, secular as well as religious authority seems to have been exercised by the Community of Saint Cuthbert, the successors of the displaced monks of Lindisfarne, who after many years of wandering with Cuthbert's remains established a permanent capital at Durham in 995. They had originally been granted the territory by King Guthfrith of York in the 880s, so they considered themselves to be outside the jurisdiction of either the English or Norse kings. This anomalous situation eventually led to the recognition in the fourteenth century of Durham as a County Palatine, which was part of the Kingdom of England but remained effectively the personal possession of the Bishops of Durham. North of the Tyne, in present-day Northumberland, a line of self-styled native kings continued to rule from Bamburgh, sometimes as clients of the kings in York, at other times effectively independent. After the collapse of the Norse regime, York and Northumbria came under the control of ealdormen (later styled earls), senior officials appointed by the English monarchs, of whom the first to be documented is Oswulf of Bamburgh. Over the next half century, a succession of earls of Northumbria, alternatively known as the earls of Bamburgh, operated as de facto independent rulers, although in theory at least they now owed allegiance to the kings of England.

We know very little about the political background to the Battle of Carham, but it is often thought to have led to the establishment of a permanent border between Scotland and England along the River Tweed – in other words, a border almost identical to the present one. Indeed, as long ago as the 1940s, Sir Frank Stenton pointed out the likelihood that the Tweed had already been the de facto boundary for almost half a century (Stenton, 1968; updated version edited after Stenton's death). Roger of Andover, who was writing in the thirteenth century but seems to have had access to records now lost, tells us that when the Scottish King Kenneth made his submission to Athelstan's great nephew, Edgar, in 973, he was granted all the lands between the Tweed and the Forth, which in theory had previously been part of Northumberland. Stenton argued that, although no more contemporary source alludes to this grant, Roger's statement 'deserves to be taken seriously' since he had no obvious motive for inventing it. It is also indirectly supported by Symeon of Durham, who says that the English army which fought the Scots at Carham was recruited from the country between the Tees and Tweed. This suggests that the people living further north, who would have been ideally placed to attend a muster along the Tweed, were no longer subject to the authority of the earls at Bamburgh. (These questions, together with a great deal of recent research on the Battle of Carham, are discussed at more length in McGuigan and Woolf, 2018.) Certainly by the early eleventh century, the Scots had recovered from their defeats at the hands of Athelstan, and were once again pushing southwards. Malcolm II (or Mael Coluim mac Cinaeda in Gaelic), a descendant of Constantin mac Aeda, seized the throne in 1005, and in the following year, according to the *Annals of Ulster*, he invaded Northumbria. It had long been the custom of Scottish rulers to inaugurate their reigns with an attack on one of their neighbours, in order to establish their military credentials and give their supporters an opportunity to enrich themselves with loot. Malcolm got as far as Durham, which he besieged, but he was defeated by the then Earl of Bamburgh, Uhtred, son of Waltheof. The latter seems to have defended his earldom successfully for the next decade, as we hear of no more incursions from the north, but his situation changed dramatically in 1016 when Danish Prince Cnut, supported by the Danish settlers who remained in England, overthrew the English King Edmund Ironside and took the throne. Uhtred remained loyal to Edmund, and was campaigning with him in the English Midlands when the Danes invaded Northumbria. The *Anglo-Saxon Chronicle* tells us that he hurried home and was forced to submit to Cnut. It was probably the news of these disorders across the border that encouraged Malcolm to look southwards again, and ultimately led to the clash at Carham.

Uhtred's role has led to controversy regarding the exact date of the battle, because all the sources which specify a date place it in 1018 (McGuigan and Woolf), while one, Symeon of Durham's *Historia Regum*, specifically names him as the English commander. But the entry in the *Anglo-Saxon Chronicle* for 1016 goes on to say that despite Uhtred's submission to Cnut, 'nevertheless he was killed by the advice of Ealdorman Eadric' and the earldom given to another claimant. The implication is of course that Uhtred was killed some time in the same year, so either the battle took place earlier than 1018 or the *Historia Regum* is mistaken when it places him there. Stenton tended to favour the first solution and dated the battle to 1016, on the grounds that 'names are better remembered than dates', so it is more likely that one chronicler made an error with the latter than that another named a man who was not present. However, Stenton also cites one of the best pieces of evidence for a later date, which is Symeon's assertion that Bishop Ealdred died only a few days after learning of the English defeat, having completed twenty-four years at Durham Cathedral. We know that Ealdred had arrived at Durham in 995, so that would give the date of the battle as 1019. An error of a year in the chronology is quite plausible, especially as we do not know the precise date of the bishop's arrival, but for Symeon's calculation to be three years out seems much less likely. A third solution to the dating problem was suggested by A.A.M. Duncan in the 1970s and has recently been supported by Neil McGuigan. The *Anglo-Saxon Chronicle* does not actually say that 1016 was the year of Uhtred's death; rather, the annalist may have mentioned it under the entry for that year to point out the injustice of it, because it was then that the earl had made his submission to Cnut. He may have subsequently fallen from favour and been murdered, but this could have happened several years later. This hypothesis has the advantage that it leaves us free to follow our sources and accept the later date.

We can be more confident of the general location of the battle, since the same sources all agree that the Scots defeated a Northumbrian army somewhere on the banks of the River Tweed. Essentially, there are two independent sources for the conflict, but they do not give enough detail to enable us to pinpoint the exact site. It may actually have taken place on what is now the Scottish side of the river, but even if that was the case, its inclusion in this volume is surely justified because of its very great importance to border history. Fortunately, a great deal of new information and a number of fresh interpretations have been published recently, thanks to the programme of research undertaken by the Carham Society to commemorate the one thousandth anniversary of the battle (McGuigan & Wood, 2018). To begin with the written sources, the first consists of a number of versions of John of Worcester's *Chronicon ex Chronicis* produced in northern England in the early twelfth century. The original *Chronicon* was apparently completed at Worcester in the 1130s, and, as might be expected from the location of its author in the English Midlands, is not particularly interested in Northumbrian affairs, making no mention of Carham. However, large parts of John's text were copied into later works by northern writers, who frequently added additional material relevant to the history of the border regions. These works included the *Chronicle of Melrose*, the *Historia Regum* attributed to Symeon of Durham and the *Chronica* of Roger of Howden, who worked in the dioceses of Durham and Glasgow. Under the year 1018, Roger inserted a single sentence, apparently derived from the *Melrose Chronicle*, which states: '*Ingens bellum inter Anglos et Scottos apud Carrum geritur*' ('A great battle is fought between the English and the Scots at Carham'). The *Historia Regum* adds a little detail to this bald notice, giving the names of the commanders as Uhtred, Earl of Northumbria, for the English, and on the Scottish side Malcolmum filium Cyneth, or Malcolm II, King of the Scots, and Eugenius Calvus, King of Strathclyde. Eugenius Calvus ('Owen the Bald', or Owain Foel in Welsh) does not appear in the other sources, but the name Owain is known to have been associated with the royal house of Strathclyde, and another Owain, perhaps his predecessor, is referred to in Welsh records as having been killed in 1015 (Edmonds, 2018).

Eugenius is given the same title ('rex') as Malcolm, which might imply that they were of equal rank, but the precise nature of their relationship is not clear. The Kingdom of Strathclyde was related culturally and linguistically to the kingdoms of early medieval Wales. Indeed, it was often referred to in Welsh writings as Yr Hen Ogledd, or 'The Old North', implying that it was seen as a northern extension of a Welsh cultural area which had once covered much of north-west England and south-west Scotland. The name Strathclyde had originally been restricted to the immediate vicinity of its first capital, at Dumbarton Rock on the River Clyde, but by the 940s it had expanded to include not only what is now Galloway in south-western Scotland, but the Welsh-speaking regions of modern Cumbria. The people of Strathclyde were longstanding enemies of the Angles of Northumbria, and since the end of the eighth century they had been taking advantage of the Viking attacks which had weakened their eastern neighbours to expand their own power. It is not certain to what extent they were independent of the Scottish kingdom based further north, but Fiona Edmonds argues that pressure from their neighbours in both east and west would in any case have eventually driven their rulers into an alliance with the Scots. For not only were the Northumbrians returning to the offensive, but the mixed Norse-Gaelic people known as the Gall Gaidhil were beginning a series of incursions from the west, which over the course of the next century were to turn Galloway into a Gaelic-speaking enclave (Woolf, 2007). McGuigan argues that there is no compelling evidence that Strathclyde was not an independent polity at this time, but it is perhaps noteworthy that the contemporary Irish annals describe the Scottish king as 'Ard Ri', or 'High King', which in Ireland implied overlordship over a number of lesser 'kings'. So while it is possible that there were two independent armies in the field against the Northumbrians, it is equally likely that the Strathclyde men and their leader turned out in fulfilment of some sort of obligation to the Scottish monarch.

The second independent source for the battle comprises a set of other works associated with Symeon of Durham, but which describe events from the point of view of the Bishop of Durham, Ealdhun, who may perhaps have been the original source for this material. The *Libellus de Exordio*, written about a century after the events described, tells of a great comet that was seen over Northumbria for thirty days prior to the battle and states that the battle was a disastrous defeat for the Northumbrians. Almost all the people living between the rivers Tees and Tweed were said to have been killed in the fight. Upon learning of the disaster, the bishop was said to have lamented: 'Oh why was I spared to see these times?' The *Annals of Lindisfarne and Durham* add that he was so stricken with grief that he died soon afterwards. McGuigan mentions two other possible sources of information, but these cannot be shown to be definitely independent of the first two. One Scottish king list tells us briefly that Mael Coluim mac Cinaeda 'fought a great battle at Carrun', but this list dates from around the end of the twelfth century, by which time Roger of Howden's work had already become a much-quoted source for Scottish history. The remaining possibility is that the fourteenth-century *Chronica Gentis Scotorum* of John of Fordun was referring to Carham when it describes a battle 'near Burgum' in which Mael Coluim defeated Uhtred. But McGuigan argues that the only plausible locations for 'Burgum' are at Burgh by Sands and Brough under Stainmore, which are both in Cumbria on the western side of the Pennines. The village of Birgham, which is located on the northern bank of the Tweed opposite Carham, was originally Bricgham (Old English for 'Bridgetown'), a word which is unlikely to have been confused with 'Burgh', meaning a fortified place. So either John of Fordun is describing another, otherwise unknown battle, or one of his sources has transferred the location to Cumbria. This is perhaps more likely than it might seem, because a Scottish claim to that county was being energetically pursued when John wrote in the thirteenth century, and he or his informant may have felt that a historic Scottish victory there would help to legitimize the claim.

None of these writers give us any information about the size of the opposing forces, and the terrain over which they fought is also uncertain, which makes it difficult for us to reconstruct the course of events. We can, however, glean some information from other sources about the nature of the armies and their style of combat. The Battle of Maldon was fought in August 991, far to the south beside the Blackwater River in Essex, and it is known to us mainly from the surviving parts of an anonymous early English poem. The battle saw an English army under Ealdorman Byrhtnoth of Essex defeated by Vikings, whom the *Anglo-Saxon Chronicle* says were led by a man named Olaf. The poem cannot be treated as an infallible eyewitness account, especially as there were few English survivors, but it is likely that its description of the way battles were fought is broadly accurate, especially as its intended audience would have been local men of the warrior class, who may have known relatives or comrades who had died in the fight, even if they had not been there themselves. So we can assume that the experience of Uhtred's men at Carham would not have been very different. They would have fought on foot: the first order that Byrhtnoth gives in the fragment of the poem that we have is to send away the horses to a safe place – I rely here on Stephen Pollington's translation (Pollington, 2006, Appendix III). Then the ealdorman rides along the front of the army and ensures that everyone knows how to stand in line and hold his shield correctly, before dismounting himself and taking his place among his personal followers. He next engages in an exchange of challenges with the enemy, defiantly refusing their demand for tribute and offering instead to send them spearpoints. The tidal river lies between the armies and an English champion holds the only bridge, preventing the enemy from getting into hand-to-hand combat, but both sides shoot arrows at the other, which inflict casualties at a distance. At this point the Vikings ask Byrhtnoth to allow them to cross the river so that they can decide the battle with hand strokes. The over-confident ealdorman obliges them and orders his men to form a 'war wall' of shields to prevent the enemy from breaking through their line. Battle is then joined in earnest. 'File hardened spears' are thrown, men armed with bows keep shooting into the melee at close range, and sword and spear points clash with shields. Men on both sides are cut down; an Englishman named Eadweard fells a Viking with a single mighty blow of his sword. Others are wounded by spears, including Byrhtnoth himself, who is weakened by loss of blood and then killed by a group of Vikings who want to take his jewellery and expensive sword. Two of his bodyguards die trying to save him, but others – their names are given by the poet as if to publicly shame them – take to flight upon seeing their leader dead. One, a certain

Godric, steals Byrhtnoth's horse to make his escape. However, others decide to fight on and avenge their leader, even though their cause is now hopeless. The poet recounts their heroic deeds and equally heroic speeches as they declare their determination never to flee. Some continue to throw spears, while others draw their swords and break into the enemy formations until they are surrounded and killed; one, a Northumbrian hostage 'from a hard kindred', shoots arrows for as long as he can still fight. Some of his missiles hit the Viking shields, but others get through and strike their targets, many of whom are wounded. The poem as we have it ends with the dwindling band of Englishmen continuing the struggle, which will presumably soon end in their deaths.

If these tactics were more or less standard for English armies, it is less certain that the same applied to the Scots. Ian Heath (1979) argued that by the tenth century, Scottish fighting techniques were no different from those of the English, and that the Scots at the Battle of Brunanburgh were 'in no way distinguishable from their Viking allies in tactics'. However, the Vikings themselves seem to have disagreed. According to *Egil's Saga*, King Athelstan had summed up the typical Scottish style of fighting on the eve of the battle with the following words: 'the Scots tend to break ranks,' he warned, 'run back and forth and appear in different places. They often prove dangerous if you do not keep on the alert, but retreat if you confront them.' The carved figures on the standing stones at Aberlemno near Forfar – now generally believed to have been produced in the ninth century – and the roughly contemporary Sueno's Stone near Forres depict warriors who may well have been suited to such mobile skirmishing tactics. These stones are usually described as 'Pictish', but they probably date from around the time of the founding of the Scottish kingdom and the men represented on them may not have looked very different from their descendants who fought at Carham. Many of them are fast-moving horsemen, who wear helmets and sometimes appear to be throwing spears. Those on foot are unarmoured, bare headed and armed with small round shields and a mixture of spears and swords.

One man on the stone known as Aberlemno Two appears to have slung his shield over his shoulder and is wielding a spear in two hands as if to ward off an approaching cavalryman. Another figure, carved on a cross slab at Ardchattan Priory near Oban and thought to date from the tenth century, holds a short spear and an unusual H-shaped shield (see the Historic Environment Scotland website at canmore.org, image number E77115). This would seem to be more suited for open-order fencing, with the projections at top and bottom designed to catch or deflect enemy weapons, than for fighting in close order with overlapping shields in the English or Viking style. We cannot be certain that these differences in equipment necessarily reflected important variations in tactics, but if the Scots were more mobile than their opponents, and in particular if they included significant numbers of mounted men, it might explain why the English losses were said to be so heavy, as they would have found it difficult to outdistance their pursuers once their battle line was broken. Of course it is also possible, to judge from the example of Maldon, that at least some of the English warriors may have preferred to fight to the death rather than risk their reputations by fleeing. Nevertheless, Uhtred apparently survived the defeat, assuming that he was there at all, since none of our sources mentions his death in the battle.

Neither do they tell us anything of the subsequent career of Eugenius (or Owain) of Strathclyde, so it is possible that he was killed at Carham, but that can only be speculation. Malcolm II eventually made peace with Cnut and reigned until 1034, being described in the Scottish kings lists by such epithets as 'victorious' and 'glorious', which may reflect the enduring fame of his victory. How important it really was in political terms is uncertain. Foster (2014) notes that the period between the deaths of the Scottish kings Constantin II *c.* 945 and Malcolm II in 1034 is very sparsely illuminated by both historical and archaeological evidence, but that we can be fairly certain that by around 1018 the kingdom's southern boundary had been pushed south to roughly its present location along the rivers Tweed and Solway. In the absence of documentary evidence – for example, the text of a peace treaty between the kings of Scots and the earls of Northumberland – it cannot be proved that this expansion happened as a result of the Battle of Carham. Such a decisive victory in the vicinity of the border must at the very least have helped to consolidate Scotland's gains in that direction, but the frontier remained a fairly fluid concept for some centuries to come. The Kingdom of Scotland continued to claim extensive lands to the south of the Tweed boundary, including at various times the counties of Northumberland, Cumberland and Westmorland, and during the chaotic reign of King Stephen (1135–54) in England, David I, the King of Scots, managed to extend his power as far south as the River Ribble in Lancashire. It was not until 1237 that the Treaty of York formally established the boundary along the line of the Tweed, and even then the notorious debatable lands, on the west coast near Carlisle, remained in dispute until 1552.

The best way to get an impression of the general area where the battle was fought is to take the B6350, which runs west from the Collingwood Arms south of Coldstream through Wark and Carham villages in the direction of Kelso, or alternatively to follow the River Tweed on foot along its northern bank by paths from Coldstream itself. The Scottish bank is on the whole higher and provides better views. A telephone box in Carham village has been converted into a miniature visitor centre (grid reference NT798383), with maps and other information on the battle and border history in general. A sign outside nearby St Cuthbert's Church states that 'The Battle of Carham was fought near this place in 1018', and further information panels can be found inside the church. The Battlefields Trust has produced a thirty-minute video, *Carham 1018 – The Start of the Border Story*, which shows many of the places which may be associated with the battle and is available on Youtube.

Chapter Two

Two Battles at Alnwick, 1093 & 1174

Date	13 November 1093
Location	outside Alnwick, Northumberland
Combatants	Scots commanded by Malcolm III, King of Scots, versus English under Robert de Mowbray, Earl of Northumberland
Outcome	English victory

Date	13 July 1174
Location	Alnwick, Northumberland
Combatants	Scots under William I, King of Scotland, versus English led by Ranulf de Glanville, Sheriff of Westmorland
Outcome	English victory

AFTER THE DEATH of Uhtred, the earls of Northumbria continued to rule the region as semi-independent clients of the English kings. In 1055, Tostig Godwinson, the brother-in-law of King Edward the Confessor and brother of Edward's eventual successor, Harold Godwinson, was appointed as earl. However, he proved to be an unpopular ruler, and ten years later he was deposed at the instigation of his brother. When Harold succeeded Edward to the throne early in 1066, Tostig gave his support to Harold Hardrada of Norway, who also had a claim to the land of England, derived from Harthacnut, the son of Cnut. On 20 September 1066, Tostig defeated an English army led by Earl Edwin of Mercia and his brother, Morcar, at Fulford, outside York, but only five days later King Harold arrived and smashed Harold Hardrada's Norwegian army at Stamford Bridge. The Norwegian king was killed, together with Tostig, and the earldom of Northumbria was awarded to Morcar. However, a third claimant to the English throne, Duke William of Normandy, was already on the move. Three days after the Battle of Stamford Bridge, William landed on the south coast of England and Harold was obliged to take his men south by forced marches to confront him. Edwin and Morcar were not with him. There have been insinuations of treachery ever since, but the reasons for their absence are not clear. Perhaps Harold deliberately left them behind to guard against another invasion of the North, or possibly their forces were simply not battle-ready after their losses at Fulford. But when Harold was killed and his army scattered by Norman forces at Hastings on 14 October, almost the whole of the southern English aristocracy died with him. On 25 December, William was crowned King William I of England in Westminster Abbey. Edwin and Morcar were now the most powerful Englishmen left in the kingdom, but their resistance to the Normans was at best half-hearted. In 1068, William deprived Morcar of the earldom of Northumbria in favour of Gospatric of Bamburgh, a grandson of Uhtred, and Morcar and his brother attempted to raise the people of Mercia and the North in revolt. Their declared intention was to expel the Normans and replace William with Edgar the Aetheling, a descendant of King Edgar. Bleddyn ap Cynfyn, King of Gwynedd in North Wales, who had been a client of Edward the Confessor, also joined the campaign against William, but the rebellion collapsed almost as soon as the Normans advanced into Mercia. In the aftermath of the revolt, Gospatric, who had supported the rebels despite enjoying the king's favour, was replaced as earl by a Norman knight, Robert de Comines. The *Anglo-Saxon Chronicle* writes of Robert receiving 'the earldom over Northumberland', marking the transition around this time of the semi-independent former kingdom of Northumbria to the English county known henceforth as Northumberland.

In 1069, a fresh series of revolts broke out in the North, in the first of which Robert de Comines was killed at Durham. Then in September, a Danish army landed in Yorkshire and gained the support of disaffected locals in an attack on York. The Danes eventually withdrew, but William seems to have been so alarmed by the interminable uprisings that he embarked on a campaign with the aim not just of punishing the rebels, but of making it impossible for the region ever again to present a threat to Norman power. The ensuing Harrying of the North, as it came to be known, was presented in later chronicles as an unprecedented disaster for the region. The Worcester manuscript of the *Anglo-Saxon Chronicle* says that the Norman army 'wholly ravaged and laid waste the shire', presumably meaning the North Riding of Yorkshire, which seems to have suffered the worst destruction. Orderic Vitalis (Chibnall, 1990) claims that the king's intention was to make 'the whole region north of the Humber' uninhabitable, to which end he had his men gather together all the crops, livestock and other food supplies and destroy them. As result, says Orderic, 100,000 people starved to death. This would amount to more than one person in every twenty living in England at the time, which must be an exaggeration, but other sources confirm that there was a famine around the time of William's campaign, whether or not that was the sole cause. John of Worcester and Symeon of Durham both alleged that people ate all the horses, dogs and cats before resorting to cannibalism, and that starving refugees from the North fled as far as Evesham in Worcestershire (Groom, 2022). However the true extent of the damage is difficult to assess, and it has been questioned whether the Normans, whose presence in the country was still fairly tenuous, could have deployed the manpower needed to destroy entire counties (Dalton, 2002). Sixteen years later, the *Domesday Book* records about 300 settlements in and around Yorkshire, with a noticeable concentration in the North Riding, as 'waste' ('*vasta est*'), and many others as worth far less than they had been in the time of King Edward, but the question of exactly what was meant by 'waste', and how far the situation was caused by the king's scorched earth policy, has long been controversial. Symeon of Durham, it should be noted, mentions a number of Scottish raids during this period, which must also have contributed to the devastation. It might further be questioned whether any amount of damage, short of complete depopulation over a wide area leading to the extensive regrowth of forest, could have made fertile farmland unproductive for as long as sixteen years. Northumberland, Durham and the other border counties were not included in the *Domesday Book*, so there is a lack of evidence for the lasting effects, if any, of the Harrying north of the River Tees.

In any case, Northumberland had its own problems. The victory at Carham may have consolidated Scottish control north of the Tweed, but it did not result in stability along the border in the long term. The middle decades of the eleventh century were a turbulent time in Scotland. Malcolm II was followed by his grandson, Duncan, who was succeeded (and possibly killed) by his cousin, MacBeth, in 1040. Then in 1058, Malcolm III, known in Gaelic as 'Ceann mor' (usually Anglicized as Canmore) or 'great chief', killed MacBeth's stepson and successor, Lulach, and seized the throne for himself. During his thirty-five-year reign, Malcolm established a dynasty that would rule Scotland until the end of the thirteenth century, and his marriage to the English princess, Margaret, encouraged the introduction of Anglo-Norman and continental influences in the realms of the Church and government, but this did not lead to any lasting improvement in relations with his southern neighbour. Indeed, Malcolm repeatedly sought to push his frontier still further south whenever the political situation in England provided an opportunity, although in 1072, following William's operations in the north of England, he was obliged to agree to a peace treaty with his southern neighbour which later English monarchs were only too keen to interpret as an admission of their own superior status. Gospatric managed to hold on to his base at Bamburgh until the same year, when he defected to the Scots and was rewarded by Malcolm with a castle at Dunbar. Another Englishman, Waltheof of Northampton, was installed as earl following the death of Robert de Comines, and

King William began allocating lands in the northern counties to his loyal followers, who were expected to build castles and help to keep the people in subjection. By 1135 there were twenty-one of these 'baronies' in Northumberland, each controlled by a baron who held it as a tenant of the king in return for military service (Lomas, 1996). Humbler folk were also enlisted in the work of securing the frontier. The *Anglo-Saxon Chronicle* tells us that in 1092, William's successor, William II, resettled large numbers of peasants around a newly built castle at Carlisle on the west coast, no doubt with the aim of establishing a local source of supplies and revenue as well as a barrier against further Scottish incursions.

In 1091, a Scottish army had advanced as far as Durham, but retreated when William II came north with an army. A brief peace was agreed, and according to the *Anglo-Saxon Chronicle*, Malcolm paid homage to William and 'became his man', on the same terms as he had done with his father in 1072. However, the peace was broken again in the following year, when an army led by Malcolm in person crossed the Tweed and besieged Alnwick. The name 'Alnwick' is Old English, which implies that the settlement dates from pre-Norman times, but the first notice of it in written documents appears to be in 1093, when Malcolm's army arrived. Like Carlisle, it was one of the towns which rose to prominence as a result of the Anglo-Norman kings' attempts to bring the border region under their direct control. Alnwick was a market town on the River Aln, which lay roughly 30 miles south of the mouth of the Tweed and a similar distance north of the Tyne. It was the centre of the largest of the Anglo-Norman baronies in the borders, and the man who held it owed the king the service of twelve knights (Lomas). Most sources (see for example the Alnwick Castle website at www.alnwickcastle.com) state that the castle there was built by Yvo de Vescy, to whom William II gave the town in 1096, which raises the question of what sort of structure it was that Malcolm had besieged three years earlier. It seems unlikely that a settlement of this size would have been walled, so the logical assumption is that there was an earlier wooden castle, perhaps dating from as early as the 1070s, which de Vescy rebuilt in stone.

The Earl of Northumbria in 1093 was Robert de Mowbray, a Norman who had succeeded Aubrey de Coucy in 1086, the year of William the Conqueror's death. Orderic Vitalis describes Mowbray as a formidable character 'of great stature, strong, swarthy and hairy'. A bold and cunning warrior, 'stern and grim', he was inclined to despise his peers and disobey his feudal superiors, and he had already been in trouble with William II for supporting William's elder brother, Robert of Normandy, in his claim to the throne after their father's death. Nevertheless, he had been pardoned and reinstated as earl, and at the time of Malcolm's invasion he was at Bamburgh Castle with what seems to have been a very small retinue of knights. But in order to reach Alnwick, the Scots had had to bypass Bamburgh, which placed Mowbray in their rear. It is probable that Malcolm lacked the siege equipment necessary to attack such a fortification, but by failing to blockade it, or even leave a detachment to keep its garrison under observation, he had left himself vulnerable to a surprise attack. In doing so, he allowed the Normans the freedom to do what they did best.

Norman Cavalry Tactics

During the second half of the eleventh century, the Normans had embarked on an extraordinary period of conquest which had already taken them as far afield as Sicily, and was soon to go even further under the banner of the First Crusade, which was proclaimed by Pope Urban II in 1096. In 1081, at the Battle of Durazzo (or Dyrrhachium) in what is now Albania, they had even defeated the army of the Byzantine Empire, the greatest power in Europe at the time. One reason for this spectacular success was that the Normans had perfected a style of fighting which combined shock and mobility to an extent previously unseen in Western Europe (Gravett, 1993). Archers, crossbowmen and other foot-soldiers were employed – all of which played a prominent part in the victory at Hastings, for example – but the main striking force comprised the mounted knights. Not all heavily armoured cavalry belonged to the class of knights, but by the end of the eleventh century, the non-knightly riders – known as '*servientes*' or sergeants – seem to have been as well equipped as their superiors and fought in the same formations. The usual contemporary term for armoured cavalrymen of all ranks was '*milites*' (singular '*miles*'), from the Latin for a soldier, although in practice only the wealthy could afford the equipment needed to serve in the cavalry. A Norman *miles* wore a long iron mail coat or hauberk, and carried a sword, lance and heavy kite-shaped shield. The most expensive item in this panoply was the coat of mail, which could consist of as many as 50,000 interlocking rings and take 100 days to make (Woosnam-Savage, 2017). This inevitably placed it out of reach for the average soldier, and so tended to increase the dominant role of the upper classes in early medieval warfare.

In most respects, the knight resembled a contemporary English, Scottish or Scandinavian noble warrior, except that he was trained to fight on horseback. Cavalry of course was not new, but the Normans were well ahead of their rivals in combining its advantages of shock and mobility. Apart from the obvious bonus of greater speed, the extra height and momentum provided by the horse gave a man an advantage in hand-to-hand combat, but against this was the tendency of cavalry to advance in a disorderly mob, with men either falling behind or galloping ahead unsupported, according to the fitness of their horses and their own desire or ability to control them. Much has been made of the question of whether the lance in this era was used overarm or couched, in other words tucked under the rider's arm to enable him to deliver a thrust with the weight of the horse behind it. An overarm thrust was weaker as it relied solely on the strength of the wielder's arm, but it allowed him to move it more easily to face threats coming from different directions, as well as giving the option of throwing the lance if he could not advance close enough for a thrust, for example if the opponent was using a longer weapon. The Bayeux Tapestry shows the Normans using their lances overarm at Hastings, but the situation in that battle was particularly unsuitable for a charge to close quarters because the English were deployed on top of a steep hill and were armed with long-handled axes which could easily kill the Normans' horses. Probably more important than the method of employing the lance was the ability of Norman horsemen to attack at speed while in close order, so that the maximum number of lance points could be brought to bear against the enemy, while preventing him from outflanking isolated men or pushing forward through gaps in the formation. This naturally required intensive training in weapon handling and horsemanship, but as professional warriors, who were able to delegate farming and other routine tasks to their inferiors, the *milites* were able to devote the time to do this. Their manoeuvres were further facilitated by deploying in small companies, or '*conrois*', of perhaps twenty-five to fifty men each (Gravett, 1993), which could be kept together much more easily than a long and unwieldy battle line. We do not know exactly how these units were commanded, although we do have evidence of what might happen if the job was not done properly; Orderic Vitalis, describing Geoffrey of Anjou's campaign in Normandy in 1136, remarks that the great lords 'ought to have led separate squadrons in a properly levied army'. Their failure to do so, he suggests, was a major factor in the failure of the operation.

Close order was maintained by advancing at a trot until the final hundred yards or less, then spurring the horses into a brief gallop for the final onslaught. If two opposing forces of *milites* clashed head-on at the gallop, the result would have been mutual annihilation, with men and horses all going down in a confused heap. Therefore, such an engagement must have resembled a game of 'chicken', with each side hoping that the other's nerve would fail at the last moment, prompting them to swerve aside. If this did not happen, they would have reined in their horses and finished the charge at a slow trot or walk, eventually coming to a halt and fencing with swords or lances in search of an opportunity to thrust at an unguarded opponent, but losing their advantage of mobility by doing so. By the twelfth century, it was common for a Norman army which was outnumbered or otherwise uncertain of victory to avoid these undesirable consequences by dismounting and holding off hostile horsemen with their spears, supported by infantry archers, while a small cavalry reserve manoeuvred itself into position to charge the flanks or rear of the enemy. But when the cavalry charge could be delivered against a target which was less cohesive and disciplined, or was not prepared to receive it, it was virtually unstoppable. Anna Comnena, writing of the First Crusade, famously remarked that a charging knight could knock a hole in the walls of Babylon, while Muslim chronicler Abu Shamah complained that a 'Frank' in his armour resembled a 'block of iron', and would never fall unless you first killed his horse (Heath, 1978).

The Scottish kings had been employing Normans as mercenaries since the reign of MacBeth in the middle of the eleventh century, but they never had enough of them to be able to meet the Anglo-Normans on equal terms, and in any case most of their country was unsuitable for raising the big war horses that were needed to carry them (Matthew Strickland, 'The Kings of Scots at War, *c*.1093–1286', in Spiers, Crang & Strickland, 2012). There may have been no more than a hundred knights' fees (A 'knight's fee' was a unit of land that was considered to be sufficient to support a knight, along with his horses, equipment, etc. It was not a fixed unit of area because land naturally varies in its productivity, but is useful because it places a rough upper limit on the number of knights that a country could support.) in the whole of Scotland at this time, and we have no information on how many of these knights, if any at all, accompanied Malcolm in 1093. Neither do we know the composition of the rest of his army, but the best indication might be the much better-documented Scottish force that fought in the Battle of the Standard in North Yorkshire, forty-five years later in 1138. The old Pictish-style light cavalry seem to have disappeared, but the infantry were still lightly armed and mobile, much like their predecessors at Brunanburgh, and consequently lacking in order and discipline. According to Henry of Huntingdon (Greenway, 1996), their English opponents mocked them as 'unarmed and naked', and although we should probably not take the term 'naked' too literally, Ailred of Rievaulx confirms that even their leaders disdained the use of armour. At the Standard, the men of Galloway, and probably those of Lothian as well (Henry of Huntingdon appears to confuse the two), charged furiously with swords, javelins and long spears, but their lack of any protection left them hopelessly vulnerable to English archery. Men like this, although effective enough in ambushes and swift attacks in difficult terrain, stood little chance against the Normans in a battle in the open.

The First Battle of Alnwick

On the north bank of the River Aln, on the opposite side from the town, the ground rises gently for about half a mile. At the top of the slope is a strip of woodland running north-west to south-east, and it was in the vicinity of this wood that the Scottish army set up its camp. Today there is a small roundabout there, where the B6341 going north from Alnwick meets a minor road coming from the east. Of course, although the area was partly forested in 1093, just as it is now, the precise locations of the wooded areas need not have borne any relation to those of the present day, and it is likely that the area where the Scots were camped was open country at the time, though perhaps near enough to the trees to provide a convenient supply of firewood. This location should have provided a good view of the country to the north, but the *Anglo-Saxon Chronicle* is clear that when Mowbray's attack came it took Malcolm by surprise. The date, according to John of Worcester, was St Brice's Day, 13 November, so there may not have been many leaves still on the trees. The approach of the Normans could nevertheless have been concealed by dense woodland, or it is possible that the Scots were simply careless about posting sentries. Whatever the reason, if they had not had time to draw up their men in battle formation, their chances of stopping a Norman cavalry charge – slim at the best of times – were reduced to zero. We have no eyewitness accounts of the ensuing fight, but it seems likely that many of the Scots would have scattered immediately, while any small groups that tried to make a stand would have been quickly ridden down. Among the casualties were both Malcolm and his son, Edward, the heir to the throne. According to the *Anglo-Saxon Chronicle*, Malcolm was killed by Morel of Bamburgh, who was Earl Robert's steward but was also the godfather of the Scottish king. The Norman-French rhymed chronicle of Geoffrey Gaimar, written around 1136, also names one Geoffrey Engulevent, or de Gulevent, as responsible for the deed. The king may in fact have been struck several times, and naturally anyone who had managed to land a blow would claim the credit for killing him. Today, the Malcolm Cross, situated in the wood a few yards from the road junction, marks the spot where he is believed to have fallen. The modern monument bears an inscription stating that it was erected in 1774 by Elizabeth, Duchess of Northumberland, who was a descendant of the Scottish king. We are further told that it replaced a much older cross 'decayed by time', the pedestal of which survives nearby. There is therefore no reason to doubt that its location preserves a genuine memory of the event, although it appears that Malcolm was not actually killed on the field of battle, but died later of his wounds. The ruins of Saint Leonard's Hospital, which is traditionally said to have been built on the spot where he died, are about 400 yards down the hill in the direction of Alnwick. There was once a spring there, the filled-in remains of which were excavated in 1975 (see the Historic England listing for St Leonard's Hospital at historicengland.org.uk). The spring was later believed to have healing properties, and it would have been a logical place for the Scots to take their wounded after the battle.

When Queen Margaret learned of the deaths of her husband and eldest son, she was so stricken with grief that, according to the *Anglo-Saxon Chronicle*, she went to church with all her priests and prayed for death. John of Worcester adds that within three days, her prayer was granted. Malcolm was succeeded as king by his brother, Donald III, known as Donald 'Ban' or 'Fair', who was already around 60 years old and had no surviving sons. Donald's nephew, Duncan, a son of Malcolm by his first wife, invaded the kingdom in 1094 and temporarily drove out his uncle, but in November Duncan was assassinated and Donald Ban resumed the throne in alliance with one of the sons of Malcolm and Margaret, Edmund, whom he designated as his heir. The youngest of their sons, David, who was then about 12 years old, was sent to the English court to be educated – a common practice at the time, but one which in this instance had the additional advantages of removing David to safety in a time of potentially dangerous succession disputes and of providing William with a useful hostage (Oram, 2008).

Robert de Mowbray did not enjoy his triumph for long. In 1095, he joined another conspiracy against the king, this time with the aim of placing Count Stephen of Aumale on the throne. Most of the other rebels quickly came to terms with William, and Robert was left isolated in his stronghold at Bamburgh. When a royal army appeared outside the castle, Robert fled, but was later captured at Tynemouth. The *Anglo-Saxon Chronicle* says that Morel the steward had defected to the king and betrayed many of his master's fellow conspirators. Robert himself was forced to spend the rest of his life in what must to him have seemed an ignominious retirement as a monk at St Albans Abbey. Meanwhile, Edgar, another of Malcolm and Margaret's sons, had fled to the English court and gained the support of William II, who as soon as Mowbray's revolt had been suppressed sent another army to overthrow Donald Ban. This army was led by Edgar the Aetheling, the last surviving male descendant of Alfred the Great. Edgar was regarded by Anglo-Saxon loyalists as the rightful king of England, but he had made his peace with the Normans and joined them in their war against Scotland. The *Anglo-Saxon Chronicle* says that Edgar 'won that land with a fierce fight' and succeeded in placing Edgar, son of Malcolm, on the throne, 'in allegiance to the King William'. Donald Ban was blinded on Edgar's orders and died in prison, while his heir, Edmund, was exiled to a monastery. William's claim to the allegiance of the kings of Scots was to cause a great deal of trouble for the future, but for the moment England's superior status seemed to have been confirmed. Then in 1100, William was fatally shot in the New Forest in what was claimed to be a hunting accident, and was succeeded with suspicious haste by his brother, Henry I. Edgar the Aetheling continued his adventurous life by joining the First Crusade and was still alive in 1125, when he must have been in his late 70s, as William of Malmesbury described him then as living in quiet retirement.

Henry's accession initially strengthened the ties between the English and Scottish royal houses, as he was married to King Edgar's sister, Edith Matilda. It also greatly improved the standing of the young prince, David, who as the brother of the English queen received a number of valuable titles and estates in both kingdoms, including the earldom of Huntingdon. Indeed, after 1113 he was virtually the independent ruler of most of southern Scotland, though he was ultimately dependent on English support to deter his brother, Alexander, who had succeeded Edgar as King of Scots in 1107, from exerting his authority. David was widely regarded as an admirer of Anglo-Norman culture, which in the rather patronising phrase of William of Malmesbury had 'polished away the rust of his native barbarism' during his long stay in England. So when Alexander died childless in 1124, Henry enthusiastically supported David's claim to the Scottish throne. For the first decade of his reign, David faced numerous rebellions from dynastic rivals and elements of the Scottish nobility who distrusted his English connections (see Chapter 6 of my *King Stephen and the Anarchy*, Pen & Sword, 2018). In several of these campaigns he received significant military support from Henry. For example, at the Battle of Stracathro in 1130 the victorious royal forces were led by an Englishman, Edward Siwardsson, who was serving as Constable of Scotland, and in 1134 a group of northern English barons led by Walter Espec made an expedition into Scotland and captured David's principal rival, Malcolm mac Alasdair.

When Henry died in 1135, he was succeeded by his nephew, Stephen, whose claim to the throne was immediately disputed by Henry's daughter, Matilda. David's policy towards England soon became much more assertive, ostensibly because he supported Matilda, who was his niece, but also because he saw a new opportunity to expand his kingdom at England's expense. Early in 1138, a Scottish army crossed the Tweed and besieged the castles at Wark and Norham. These fortifications had both been constructed during Henry's reign, reflecting a growing recognition of the importance of the River Tweed as the boundary between the kingdoms. Norham was erected around 1121 by the Bishop of Durham, Ranulf Flambard, and had already been briefly held by the Scots in 1136. Wark was a more recent construction, built in 1136 by Walter Espec, who was now the High Sheriff of Yorkshire and the most powerful baron in the north of England. David took Norham but was unable to capture Wark, so he bypassed it and led his army south through Northumberland. The English chroniclers Richard of Hexham and Ailred of Rievaulx alleged that the invaders committed numerous atrocities, including the taking of slaves and the murder of priests and other non-combatants. David was a cultured man and a devout Christian, but it seems that he had little control over his army, and although some of the allegations must be exaggerated, the behaviour of the Scots was bad enough to rouse the whole of the north of England against them. King Stephen was distracted by revolts in the South, but an army was mustered under the command of Walter Espec and William of Aumale, who was later made Earl of York. On 22 August 1138, the opposing armies clashed at the Battle of the Standard, which was so called for the '*caroccio*', or wagon carrying banners and religious relics, which accompanied the English from York. The result was a victory for Espec and Aumale, and David was forced to withdraw from Yorkshire, but the northern English levies could not remain in the field long enough to exploit their success, so the Scots remained in control of large parts of northern England.

A peace was agreed which held for the rest of Stephen's reign, during which the de facto border remained further south than it had ever been before or has been since. It now ran roughly from Newcastle on the east coast to Preston in the west, although the castles at both Newcastle and Bamburgh remained in English hands. Despite the defeat at the Standard, David managed to capture and demolish the castle at Wark on his return north. The legal fiction was maintained that his son, Henry, owed allegiance to Stephen for the earldom of Northumberland, but in practice almost the whole of the county was under Scottish control. The great stronghold at Carlisle, which Henry had rebuilt in stone in the 1120s, was also held by the Scots, but even more valuable to David were the silver mines at Alston, in the hills east of Carlisle. There were no sources of the metal in Scotland itself, but his new acquisition enabled David to issue the country's first silver coinage. The situation changed drastically in the early 1150s, however. David died in 1153, and as his son, Henry, had predeceased him, he was succeeded by his 11-year-old grandson, Malcolm IV. Then in the following year, Stephen also died and the formidable Henry II, the son of Stephen's rival, Matilda, came to the English throne. Henry inherited not only England but also extensive territories on the continent – Normandy, which had been conquered by his father, Geoffrey of Anjou, during Stephen's reign, Anjou itself and the Duchy of Aquitaine, which he acquired through his wife, Eleanor. This enormous power bloc, which later became known as the Angevin Empire, gave Henry much greater resources than any of his predecessors since William the Conqueror.

The young King of Scots was no match for such an opponent, and was quickly intimidated into ceding all the lands in the north of England that his grandfather had managed to acquire. In return, Malcolm received the earldom of Huntingdon, which had once belonged to his father, but had to do homage for it to Henry, who further asserted his overlordship by knighting him in 1159. In the opinion of most contemporaries, such a ceremony implied – if it did not specifically state – a relationship of patron and client. Malcolm died childless in 1165, at the age of only 24, and was succeeded by his younger brother, William I. A much more strong-willed character than his brother, William was physically powerful and a renowned warrior, as well as an efficient administrator. Jordan Fantosme, a cleric based at Winchester who wrote in the 1180s, describes him as skilled in war but too easily swayed by his foreign advisors. William's popular nickname of 'the Lion' is not attested any earlier than the late fourteenth-century chronicle of John of Fordun, but it is not inappropriate. During a long and turbulent reign, he succeeded in extending royal control over the remote regions of Caithness, Sutherland and Galloway, which had previously been only nominally part of the Scottish kingdom. Inevitably, however, the main aim of his foreign policy was to reverse Malcolm's losses in England, and in particular to reclaim the title to Northumberland which had belonged to his father.

William's opportunity came in 1173, when Eleanor and three of their four sons rebelled against Henry. The contemporary verse chronicle of Jordan Fantosme gives a detailed account of the ensuing war (Michel, 1840). The immediate cause of the revolt was the king's apparent favouritism towards his youngest son, John, at the expense of the heir, Henry 'the Young King'. The younger Henry had actually been crowned in 1170, while his father was still alive, but this precipitated the very succession dispute that it was intended to avoid. The Young King's position excited the jealousy of his brothers, while he was himself frustrated by his father's reluctance to delegate any real power to him. Henry II's reputation had also suffered badly from his involvement in the notorious murder of the Archbishop of Canterbury, Thomas Becket, three years earlier. Now his possessions in England and Normandy were attacked simultaneously by the French, Bretons, Scots and an army of Flemish soldiers commanded by Robert de Beaumont, Earl of Leicester. The Flemings fought on foot with spears, but according to Jordan Fantosme they were mostly weavers by trade rather than soldiers, their motive for coming to England being to seize control of the lucrative wool business. The chronicler tells how Henry asked his Scottish counterpart for help. William offered to send 1,000 knights and 30,000 foot-soldiers if

Henry would recognize his right to Northumberland, but the English king refused to make any territorial concessions, which so provoked William's nobles that they urged him to take the field against Henry instead. King Louis of France, on the other hand, agreed to recognize William's claim to Northumberland in return for his intervention on the side of the rebels. A Scottish army therefore crossed the Tweed and attempted to take the castles at Wark, Newcastle and nearby Prudhoe, but was unsuccessful and soon retired back over the border. According to Fantosme, this army included contingents from as far north as Ross and Moray, many of whom were 'naked people', by which he presumably means unarmoured men like those described at the Battle of the Standard. Meanwhile, Henry's other enemies were all defeated in succession by the formidable combination of English cavalry, dismounted knights and archers. In October, Robert of Leicester was caught by a larger royalist army while crossing a river at Fornham in Suffolk and captured, and the coalition against Henry collapsed.

The revolt broke out again in the following year, however, and after Easter, William the Lion led an army which included French and Flemish mercenaries back over the border. He again besieged Wark, which was held by Roger d'Estutevile, but was unable to take it despite deploying stone-throwing artillery, archers and crossbowmen, and repeatedly sending his Flemings into assaults in which they suffered heavy losses. Raising the siege, William crossed over to the west coast, where he captured Appleby and Brough, then moved back east to Prudhoe. Finding that the castle had been reinforced, he destroyed the gardens and cornfields in the vicinity and, according to Jordan Fantosme, even damaged the bark of the apple trees in an act of petty vengeance. The frustrated Scots then moved northwards again and laid siege to Alnwick. Meanwhile, King Henry had returned to England from Normandy, where he had been orchestrating the defence of the duchy, and on 12 July, in an attempt to regain popular support as well as divine forgiveness, he performed a public penance at Canterbury for the killing of Becket. This, it seems, achieved the desired result. On the previous day, the Sheriff of Westmorland, Ranulf de Glanville, had marched from Newcastle to raise the siege of Alnwick, meeting up on the way with a contingent led by Odinel de Umfraville, the castellan of Prudhoe. Fantosme also mentions Bernard de Balliol and Roger d'Estutevile's son, William, and sixty knights sent by the Archbishop of York. It was Odinel, no doubt eager to avenge the damage done to his estates, who guided the small army through the short summer night. On the 13th, de Glanville arrived at Alnwick at the head of a combined force of perhaps 400 horsemen, to find that the enemy was completely unaware of his approach. Most of the Scots were burning and pillaging in the surrounding countryside, leaving William blockading Alnwick Castle with about 500 of his inexperienced and already battered Flemings and Frenchmen. History was about to repeat itself.

We do not know whether William was aware of the circumstances of Malcolm III's death eight decades earlier, but it seems extraordinary that he should have made the same mistake, especially as the battlefield role of knightly cavalry was even more important than it had been in 1093. Ranulf's horsemen would have looked slightly different from Robert de Mowbray's (see Heath, 1989): more of them would have been wearing mail armour to protect their legs, and their shields might have been slightly smaller as they came to rely more on their armour. A few would perhaps have been wearing fabric surcoats over their mail, a fashion which had been brought back from the Crusades. The twelfth century had seen the beginnings of the system of heraldry, so the most prominent knights may have carried the distinctive devices associated with that practice on their shields or helmets. But their style of fighting was the same, and infantry had still not developed a way of countering their deadly charge. In later centuries, the mercenary Flemish infantry were to turn the tables on the mounted knights with close-packed, disciplined phalanxes of spearmen, but Robert of Leicester's amateur contingent had been ridden down at Fornham, and William's Flemings seem to have had no influence on the events at Alnwick. In fact, William had not only failed to prepare for the possibility of an attack, he had divided his forces and sent Earl Duncan of Fife to attack Warkworth, on the coast half a day's march to the south-east. We do not know the strength of William's army; Jordan Fantosme repeatedly calls it a 'great host', but it was apparently spread out over a wide area and there seems to be no suggestion that either the Flemings or the Scots attempted to form a line of battle, or had the time to do so.

Fantosme, who claims to have been an eyewitness, says that the morning of 13 July was hot, and William had removed his helmet in order to eat before beginning an assault on the castle. The spot where he is said to have been standing when the enemy came upon him is still marked by a plaque near the entrance to Hulne Park on the outskirts of Alnwick. The English knights had been concealed in a copse while their scouts observed the Scottish dispositions, then suddenly they mounted their horses and charged, shouting their various war cries. William's reaction may have been greatly to his credit as a knight, but for an army commander – and especially for a king – it was reckless. He immediately mounted his grey horse and charged the enemy, crying out: 'Now we shall see which of us are good knights!' Some at least of the Flemings followed him and a furious fight ensued. William knocked down the first English knight he encountered, but then a sergeant disembowelled his horse with a lance thrust, and the king was thrown to the ground and pinned beneath the dead animal. There was a brief flurry of arrows and darts, presumably from the Scottish side, but then, says Fantosme, de Glanville's knights closed in with lances and swords and 'great carnage' was made of the surprised and disordered Flemings, after which the survivors fled. Ranulf de Glanville personally accepted the surrender of the Scottish king. Fantosme describes the deeds of several other Scottish knights who fought bravely before they either escaped or were captured, which suggests that the fight went on for some time, but many of the Scots must have scattered as soon as their king fell. They were pursued relentlessly by the victors. Fantosme says that more than a thousand of them were badly wounded, a catastrophe which he ascribes to God's anger at atrocities said to have been committed at Warkworth, but which would only be the expected outcome if men on foot had attempted to outrun the English cavalry.

The captive Lion was carried off in chains to Newcastle, and from there, on the orders of King Henry, he was taken to meet him at Falaise in Normandy. There, he was forced to acknowledge the English king as his feudal overlord and put his signature to a document, known as the Treaty of Falaise, by which he surrendered a number of castles and towns, including Edinburgh, Stirling, Roxburgh, Jedburgh and Berwick. As if this was not enough, William was obliged to pay the enormous sum of 40,000 Scottish marks to cover the costs of an English occupation of his country. He was then released, but upon his return home he had to contend with several revolts in Galloway and the Highlands, provoked partly by his nobles' disgust at the concessions he had been forced to make to secure his freedom. However, Henry II died in 1189, and his successor, Richard I, agreed to cancel the treaty and hand back the castles in return for another 10,000 marks. Richard's priority was to raise money for a crusade, and he was even prepared to consider a Scottish offer to buy the whole of Northumberland, but the deal did not go through because he was unwilling to surrender the castles on his side of the border, which played a vital role in protecting Durham and York. It seems that even William the Lion was inclined to see the hand of the martyred Thomas Becket in the events at Alnwick, and was anxious to ensure that his kingdom had its share of divine favour. When Arbroath Abbey was completed under his auspices in 1197, he dedicated it to St Thomas of Canterbury. William died in 1214, by which time he had left his humiliation at Alnwick behind him and become one of Scotland's most respected monarchs.

The Malcolm Cross is at grid reference NU190147, near a small roundabout where the minor road going east towards Denwick leaves the B6341 which runs north from Alnwick to join the A1 near South Charlton. The distance from Alnwick is less than a mile and the spot can easily be reached on foot. The cross is situated in a narrow strip of woodland on the right of the road when travelling away from Alnwick. The plaque commemorating the capture of King William at the Second Battle of Alnwick is not quite so easy to find. It is located at Grid Reference NU180136, about a quarter of a mile west of the castle, on Ratten Row. If you walk up Bailiffgate away from the castle, Ratten Row is on the left, 50 yards past the turning to Northumberland Street. The monument is a granite slab tucked away behind some railings on your left hand side just before the gateway leading to Hulne Park, which was once a hunting park belonging to the Percy family. The stone was erected in the nineteenth century to replace an earlier monument on the same site. The surrounding area has been extensively built up and developed since the twelfth century and it is no longer possible to identify the wood from which the English attack was launched, but it was presumably somewhere between Ratten Row and the River Alne, 300 yards away to the north.

Chapter Three

'When Barwycke Was Wonne': Berwick-upon-Tweed, the Most Fought-over Town in Britain

FOR MOST OF the period covered by this book, the town of Berwick-upon-Tweed – situated on the north bank of the River Tweed where it flows into the North Sea – functioned as a defensive stronghold and major supply base for whichever side held it at the time. The area now occupied by the town was originally part of the kingdom (and subsequently the earldom) of Northumbria; the name Berwick is English, meaning 'barley farm'. We have no documentary evidence for its early history, but it may have come under Scottish control in the aftermath of the Battle of Carham, which was fought less than 30 miles away. However it was not established as a borough and port until the reign of David I, who also undertook the building of the town's first fortifications in the second quarter of the twelfth century. During the medieval period, most of Scotland's trade and diplomatic relations were with countries bordering on the North Sea, and all of the major ports were situated on the east coast. Berwick was at one time the most prosperous of them all. It sits only 15 miles from the old seat of Northumbrian power at Bamburgh, whose castle is clearly visible today from the walls of the town. Often cited as the most fought over place in Britain, Berwick changed hands more than a dozen times between the outbreak of war between England and Scotland in 1296 and its final capture by the English in 1482.

In December 1174, Berwick was ceded to England by the Treaty of Falaise, only to be returned by Richard I fifteen years later (see Chapter Two, above). During the thirteenth century, the town prospered thanks to its seaborne trade, surpassing even Edinburgh. In 1237, Henry III of England and Alexander II of Scotland signed the Treaty of York, by which the Scots formally renounced their claim to the counties of Northumberland, Westmorland and Cumberland, but this did not affect the status of Berwick, which, being on the northern bank of the Tweed, was considered to be part of the Scottish county of Berwickshire rather than of Northumberland. In 1292, after King Alexander III had died without heirs, the town was chosen as the venue for the negotiations which ended with Edward I of England choosing John Balliol as king of the Scots. But three years later, angered by the humiliating way in which Edward treated John as his vassal, a group of Scottish nobles known as the Council of Twelve convened at Stirling and declared their new king deposed. Instead of sending troops to help the English in their war with France, as Edward had demanded, they concluded an alliance with the French and invaded northern England in support of their new ally. In March 1296, Edward retaliated. He crossed the Tweed with a large army, said to have comprised 30,000 infantry and 5,000 cavalry, and descended on Berwick (Peter, 2014). On Good Friday, 30 March, he took the town by storm and forced the garrison of the castle to surrender on terms. The ease with which the place was captured suggests that the walls, if they existed at this time, were not substantial. The common soldiers were allowed to leave, but the governor, William Lord Douglas, was imprisoned and the town was then brutally sacked. Walter Bower, who wrote his *Scotichronicon* in the 1440s, gives the total number of civilians killed as 7,500, and says that 'Edward spared no one, whatever the age or sex, and for two days streams of blood flowed from the bodies of the slain … so that mills could be turned by the flow of their blood' (Taylor *et al.*, 1987–98).

In August 1296, after defeating the Scots at the Battle of Dunbar in April, Edward returned to the town to receive the submission of most of the Scottish nobles. It was probably at this time that the earliest surviving fortifications were built, consisting of a ditch and a bank with a wooden palisade along the top (historicengland.org.uk). It is said that Edward I moved the first load of earth himself in 1296, using a wheelbarrow – a device only recently introduced into England (Creighton & Higham, 2005). No doubt this was a symbolic indication of the importance which he attached to the project. Despite all the destruction, Berwick had evidently continued to function as a town, although it had been necessary to bring in English burgesses to replace their late Scottish counterparts and keep the port operating. The English held Berwick until 1318, by which time they had greatly strengthened both the castle and the town walls, replacing the palisade with a stone curtain wall with towers at intervals and deepening the ditch into a water-filled moat protecting the northern and eastern sides of the town. This work was paid for by murage, a tax levied on imported goods which was intended specifically for the improvement or maintenance of town walls. Meanwhile, the Scots were fighting back, and after their decisive victory over Edward's ineffectual successor, Edward II, at the Battle of Bannockburn in 1314 they returned to the offensive along the border. By 1317, their king Robert I, 'the Bruce', had regained all the other castles in Scotland, and in the autumn of that year he laid siege to Berwick. He was unable to take it on that occasion, but in the following April an English burgess, Peter Spalding, who was married to a Scot, helped Bruce's leading general, Sir James Douglas, to enter the town with a force of Scottish troops. The English garrison in the castle nevertheless held out, obliging Robert to return with a siege train. The siege lasted for eleven weeks, but the defenders were eventually starved out and forced to surrender. Robert expelled the English burgesses and installed his son-in-law, Walter Stewart, as Keeper of the castle.

Edward III of England laid siege to Berwick again in 1333, retaking it in July in the aftermath of his victory at the Battle of Halidon Hill (see below, Chapter Four). It remained in English hands until November 1355, when Thomas Earl of Angus and Patrick Earl of March, leading a Scottish raid on Northumberland in support of their French allies, arrived by boat and got into the town by placing ladders over the walls under cover of darkness. In a chaotic street fight, they drove the English garrison back into the castle and captured a tower, known as the Douglas Tower, which defended the town side of the bridge which led from the town to the castle. However, they were unable to seize the castle itself so they withdrew, leaving 130 men to hold the town. It is not entirely clear whether King Edward, who was campaigning in France, learned of the fall of Berwick before he returned home, but it is possible that it was a factor in inducing him to temporarily abandon the war across the Channel. He arrived at Newcastle on Christmas Eve and began to assemble an army. Early in January 1356, an advance guard under one of Edward's leading commanders, Walter Mauny, reached Berwick and began mining operations against the walls. The Scots resisted for a few days, but when the main English army arrived they agreed to evacuate the town, which they were permitted to do. Edward went on to put further pressure on the Scots by ravaging Lothian, and in the following year a peace treaty was signed at Berwick, by the terms of which a ransom of 100,000 marks was agreed for the Scottish King David II, who had been a prisoner in England since the Battle of Neville's Cross in 1346 (see Chapter Five).

After that, the town remained in English hands until 1461, when Henry VI of England and his queen, Margaret of Anjou, fled to Scotland following their defeat by the rival Yorkist faction at the Battle of Towton. Margaret returned Berwick to Scotland in return for a pledge of support, but this was insufficient to prevent the victory of the Yorkists, who placed Edward IV on the English throne. The two countries agreed a peace treaty in 1474, but this was not popular among many in Scotland, who opposed the policies of the unwarlike King James III. Prominent among these men was James's younger brother, Alexander, the Duke of Albany. In 1480, the Earl of Angus, Archibald Douglas, attacked Bamburgh Castle, and two years later Edward IV's brother, Richard, Duke of Gloucester– the future King Richard III – marched north with 20,000 men to invade Scotland in retaliation. With him came Albany, who was now styling himself King Alexander of Scotland. The Scottish commanders in Berwick – David Lindsay, Earl of Crawford, and Andrew, Lord Gray – surrendered the town in the face of this overwhelming force, although the castle remained under the command of the Sheriff of Berwickshire, Patrick Hepburn, who refused to negotiate in spite of all Richard's threats and promises (Scott, 2023 (2)).

Richard left a detachment to invest the castle and continued his march north. The besiegers were led by Thomas, Lord Stanley, and according to the sixteenth-century writer, John Stow, they numbered 4,000 men. James III had raised an army in Edinburgh to oppose the English, but when it reached Lauder in Berwickshire his nobles mutinied and forced him to return to Edinburgh Castle. It seems likely that they took the view that under the incompetent leadership of their king they would stand no chance in a pitched battle. Not only had they deprived Richard of the decisive confrontation which he sought, but by promising to restore Albany's forfeited lands they succeeded in detaching the latter from the English alliance. Richard arrived in Edinburgh unopposed, but no longer had the strength to capture the castle. He therefore agreed to a truce, deciding to turn back towards Berwick and conclude the siege there with the aid of the considerable artillery train which he had taken into Scotland. Albany now gathered a relief force, but was too late to prevent the fall of Berwick Castle in June 1482. Some chroniclers, such as George Buchanan, state that the surrender was a negotiated one, but the *Croyland Chronicle* suggests otherwise, with its reference to 'vast slaughter and bloodshed'. Patrick Hepburn survived to become Master of the King's Household under James IV, but within a few years both of the two main antagonists in this campaign were overthrown by their own people. Richard became King of England in June 1483 after the death of Edward IV, but was defeated and killed by Henry Tudor, aided by Thomas Stanley, at the Battle of Bosworth two years later. The victor ascended the English throne as Henry VII, the founder of the Tudor dynasty. James III was killed by a rebel faction during or soon after the Battle of Sauchieburn in 1488. The latest change of ownership in

Berwick was more permanent, and it was said that in England men were proud to boast that they had been present 'when Barwycke was wonne', a phrase which became so well known that it appeared in an English–Latin dictionary as late as 1519 (Scott, 2023 (2)).

The Scots never regained the town. In 1497, their new king, James VI, allegedly proposed to Thomas Howard, the Earl of Surrey – Henry VII's lieutenant in the North – that they should decide the ownership of Berwick by single combat, but Howard prudently refused the challenge (Sadler, 2006). The Treaty of Perpetual Peace, signed in 1502 by Henry VII of England and James IV of Scotland, declared that the town's citizens were English subjects, and they and the Scots were bound not to attack or molest each other. According to the Treaty of Norham of 1551, which concluded the Eight Years' War begun by Henry VIII, Berwick was to be an independent town, legally belonging to neither side, but in practice the English garrison remained. The Scottish county of Berwickshire retained its name but thus lost its county town, which was replaced first by Greenlaw and later by Duns. Under Elizabeth I, the old town walls of Berwick were replaced with up-to-date fortifications designed in the 'trace Italienne' style, with star-shaped bastions designed to allow the entire perimeter to be covered by fire from concealed guns. These fortifications proved to be ruinously expensive and were never fully finished, but they can still be seen today, an example of sixteenth-century fortification unique in the British Isles and one of the best in Europe. Creighton and Higham make the interesting point that the area within the later fortifications is much smaller than that enclosed by Edward I's walls, which had a circuit of about 2 miles compared to the 1¼ miles of the sixteenth-century works. Consequently, a large part of modern Berwick lies outside the Elizabethan walls, but was within the circuit of the medieval defences. This is in contrast to the situation elsewhere in Britain, where if the course of the walls was ever changed it was invariably in order to accommodate an expanded urban area. (Beaumaris in Wales was a partial exception, but here the reduction of the circuit was necessary because of encroachment by the sea.) However, this need not be taken as evidence that the town of Berwick had declined in size or prosperity, since the very high cost of these unique works probably never made it feasible to protect the entire built-up area, hence priority was given to the protection of the coast and the harbour area. Seaborne attacks from Scotland were still thought to be a serious threat, as is shown by the fact that after the dissolution of the Benedictine priory on Lindisfarne in 1537, Henry VIII ordered a new castle to be built there 'against the Scots' (Tristram, 2009).

Scottish armies crossed the border again on several occasions during the civil wars of the seventeenth century, but they invariably bypassed Berwick and Elizabeth's fortifications were never tested in battle. It is worth noting, however, that one of the reasons why the Jacobite army took the western route from Scotland into England in 1745 was said to be their belief that Berwick would be a much more formidable obstacle than Carlisle (see Duffy, 2015, Chapter 9, note 29). In fact, the town's defences quickly became irrelevant after 1603, when James VI of Scotland united the two crowns upon his accession to the English throne as James I. James's main contribution to the architecture of the place was altogether less warlike. In April of that year, he travelled from Edinburgh to London (a transition which he famously described as like going from a couch of stones to a feather bed). Upon crossing the Tweed at Berwick he was shocked by the state of the wooden bridge, so in 1611 he gave £8,000 to build a new one in stone. This construction, now known as the Old Bridge, was the main route to the south from its completion in 1624 until the twentieth century.

The Act of Union of 1707 which created the United Kingdom of Great Britain made no exception for Berwick-upon-Tweed, which consequently lost its theoretically independent status by default. The Wales and Berwick Act of 1746 formalized this by defining England specifically as including Berwick. Unfortunately, this means that the well-known story that the town was at war with Russia for as long as a century after the Crimean War has no basis in fact. According to a series of newspaper stories, attested as far back as 1935, Berwick was involved in the original declaration of war by Queen Victoria in 1853, but was not mentioned in the text of the Treaty of Paris which ended the conflict in 1856 (berwickfriends.org.uk). This alarming state of affairs is variously said to have been brought to a conclusion by the British Foreign Office upon the outbreak of the First World War in 1914, or by the visit of a representative of the Soviet Union to Berwick in the 1950s. However, as the author of the 'berwickfriends' piece correctly concludes, the town was not mentioned by name in either the declaration of war or the peace treaty, and would in any case have been understood to be covered by both under the heading of 'The United Kingdom of Great Britain and Ireland'. Not surprisingly, the Foreign Office Library, which was consulted on the matter in 1965, failed to locate any documents relating to Berwick's alleged separate peace with Russia.

Today, Berwick is the most northerly town in England. It is part of the administrative county of Northumberland, but in many ways it still gives the impression of being more Scottish than English. Indeed, the nearest large city to Berwick is not Newcastle but Edinburgh. It is easily reached from either place by rail, or by road along the A1. The best places to see the remains of the medieval defences are Castle Vale Park, just south of the railway station, and at the ruins of the castle on the other side of the railway track (grid reference NT992533). The Great Hall of the castle, where Edward I set off the long wars of Scottish independence by selecting John Balliol as his puppet king, was demolished in the nineteenth century to make way for the station. James VI's Old Bridge across the Tweed is still in use, but is open only for one-way vehicle traffic owing to its restricted width.

Chapter Four

'Arrows Thick as Rays of Sunlight': Halidon Hill, 1333

Date	19 July 1333
Location	Halidon Hill, near Berwick-upon-Tweed, Northumberland
Combatants	English under Edward II, King of England, versus Scots led by Sir Archibald Douglas, Guardian of Scotland
Outcome	English victory

THE ANGLO-NORMANS HAD been victorious in both the encounters at Alnwick thanks to their superiority in heavy cavalry, but by the end of the thirteenth century the heavily armoured mounted knight was no longer the decisive weapon that he once was. However, there was nothing predetermined about this process, and it seems that it was in part the very success of English cavalry tactics that led to their demise. At the Battle of the Standard, in 1138 the English knights had mostly fought dismounted, and it has been shown that the combination of men-at-arms (descendants of the old Norman *milites*) and archers, both fighting on foot in mutual support, was already standard in the Anglo-Norman battles of the early twelfth century (Bradbury, 1985). As armour increased in weight and effectiveness during the course of the next hundred years, the charge of the heavy cavalry came to be seen more and more as the key to victory. But cavalry was usually a one-shot weapon, hard to rally once its initial charge lost momentum, and by the beginning of the fourteenth century the pendulum was swinging back once again in favour of infantry. This process was aided by the reinvention of two weapons which had already seen action in their respective armies, but had still to be developed to their full potential – the bow in England and the long spear among the Scots. After a period of several decades during which these differing approaches to warfare competed for supremacy, the issue was to be decided on a summer day in 1333 on the hills overlooking Berwick.

The English Bowmen

A once-popular view held that English archery had been relatively ineffective until the reign of Edward I, who adopted the more powerful longbow which he encountered during his campaigns in Wales in the 1280s. Jim Bradbury (1985) comprehensively demolished this theory, pointing out that English bowmen had already performed very successfully in battles such as the Standard, and that although Edward did employ Welsh archers he did not give them any special treatment (for example, they were paid less than their English equivalents) and where they fought in his armies, as at Stirling Bridge in 1297, they had little influence on the outcome. Furthermore, there is no convincing evidence from written accounts, archaeology or iconography that the bows of the fourteenth century differed in length or design from those of previous eras. The term 'longbow', often used to distinguish the medieval English and Welsh weapon from its supposedly shorter predecessors, seems not to be attested before 1448, when it appears in the *Paston Letters* in the form 'long bowe', but here it is contrasted not with some hypothetical 'short bow' but with the crossbow, which is recommended as more suitable for shooting from inside a house (Bradbury, 1985). However, by the time the Hundred Years' War broke out with France in 1337, English armies had consciously begun to develop archery as a fundamental part of their tactics, and successive governments took steps to encourage their subjects to practice the use of the bow, as well as, crucially, to establish a reliable supply of wood for bows and to organize the mass production of arrows. The best material for wooden bows, as is well known, is yew. This tree grows naturally in England, but in order to produce top-quality bow wood it needs harsher winters than are normal in the country to impose a period of dormancy each year. The Highland Scots, who relied more heavily on the bow than their Lowland compatriots, used mainly locally grown yew, of which the best came from Easragain in Argyllshire. England, however, was dependent on staves imported from continental Europe – principally Italy, Spain, Portugal and Poland – as early as the fourteenth century, and in the 1470s King Edward IV had to secure the supply by decreeing that every ship bringing in goods from Italy had to include a number of bow staves. Hardy (1992) gives numerous examples of the industrial scale of procurement which was introduced in England in order to equip and supply the archers. In 1356, no arrows were to be found in the whole of England because the king had bought up the entire supply; four years later, half a million arrows were delivered to the Tower of London in one two-month period alone. In 1417, every goose in twenty English counties had to sacrifice six feathers for fletching the arrows. Reserve supplies of missiles were packed into barrels and carried in carts; Hardy estimates that each archer might have had as many as a hundred available for his use during a campaign, which for a force of 10,000 would represent a million arrows, weighing a total of about 40 tons.

So when the English archers encountered their Scottish counterparts, there were usually many more of them, they were better drilled and trained in the mass shooting techniques appropriate to the battlefield, and they had a larger and more reliable supply of arrows. They were also probably on average from a higher social class, thus better equipped with armour, and even perhaps better nourished. It is not necessary to conclude that the Scottish bows were qualitatively inferior, though they were cheaper; 9 shillings apiece according to one sixteenth-century document, as opposed to 16 shillings for English bows (Scott, 2023). This might have been because they were slightly shorter and so used less wood, but it is perhaps more logical to suppose that it reflected their local provenance compared to expensive foreign imports. Neither is it likely that Englishmen had some innate talent for archery, but the Scottish equivalent of the yeoman who drew a bow in an English army was more likely to be wielding a spear, as specified by Robert the Bruce in 1318. According to the Statute of Arms of that date, a man owning £10 worth of goods should be equipped with a spear and a sword, with armour consisting of a helmet, gloves and either aketon or coat of mail. However, his poorer neighbour, whose possessions amounted only to the value of one cow, had to provide just a spear, or a bow with one sheaf of arrows. In England, the Statute of Winchester, enacted by Edward I in 1285, obliged the king's subjects to serve in various capacities depending on the value of the land which they held. The knights with more than £40 worth of land, and those below them in the scale with £20, served as fully armoured horsemen, while those worth £10 were to equip themselves as armoured infantry, and those with land of a value of between £2 and £5 as archers (Heath, 1982).

The precise capabilities of the medieval English longbow have been the subject of a great deal of speculation and controversy over the years. This revolves around three separate issues: the range that could be achieved, the rate of fire multiplied by the percentage of shots that hit the target, and the damage they would do if they did hit. None of these factors is susceptible to precise analysis, especially under battlefield conditions. Roger Ascham (1545) devotes considerable space to the effects of factors like temperature, humidity and especially wind; other sixteenth-century writers remark on the need for an archer to be in top physical condition to get the best out of his weapon – in contrast to firearms, which could be used just as effectively by a man who was sick, hungry or untrained – and the degrading effects of fatigue, poor rations and disease when on campaign. Ascham refers to shooting at targets at distances above fourteen score (280) yards, but implies that these ranges were only achievable in favourable weather conditions. In this connection, various versions of a 1542 law of Henry VIII are often quoted, to the effect that no archer over (or under) 24 years old was to practice shooting at a mark at less than 220 yards range (see for example Loades, 2019). But what the statute in question – the Act for the Maintaining Artillery, and the Debarring of Unlawful Games (1541) – actually says is less often examined:

> 'No Man under the age of twenty-four Years shall shoot at any standing Prick, except it be a Rover, whereat he shall change at every Shoot his Mark, upon Pain for every Shoot doing the contrary, iv d [i.e. 4 pence] and that no Person above the said Age of twenty-four Years shall shoot at any mark of eleven score yards or under, with any Prick-shaft or Flight.' (vlex.co.uk/vid/unlawful-games-act-1541-808126529).

The 1541 Act was in fact a restatement of very similar laws passed in 1511 and 1514 (Strickland & Hardy, 2005), and the text expresses a common concern of the time that men were wasting their time in gambling and other useless pastimes, at the expense of archery practice and so to the detriment of the country's military capability. No doubt it was feared that unenthusiastic archers who were forced to practice would get away with using as little effort as possible, by shooting light arrows at nearby targets. There were various approved methods of practising shooting for war. The one which we are most familiar with was shooting at the butts, which were permanent earth mounds with small targets attached, set at different ranges from the archer. Prick shooting also involved a stationary target, but usually smaller – for example a piece of white paper – and set at a shorter range. Flight shooting was shooting purely for distance, using light arrows without the heavy barbed or armour-piercing heads required for war. Roving meant moving through a demarcated area and shooting at 'rovers', a series of impromptu marks set up at different unmeasured ranges. It therefore corresponded closely to the sort of shooting that might be required when on campaign, with targets appearing unexpectedly and at unpredictable distances. The statute specified that younger men, who had perhaps not yet attained their full strength but were quicker on their feet than their elders, should accustom themselves to this sort of exercise, but with no restrictions on the range or weight of bow used. It should be noted that none of these laws ever specifies the draw weight of the bows; indeed, this method of assessing their effectiveness, so beloved of present-day longbow archers, was not employed in the days when they were actually used in war. The 1541 Act goes on to say that the older men, when using light practice arrows, should confine themselves to long-range targets, but it does not lay down any such rule for heavy war arrows. It is possible that, lacking any better system of evaluating the draw weight and power of a bow, the legislators insisted on the 220-yard limit in order to make sure that archers were using bows strong enough to achieve these distances, rather than suggesting that this was a normal engagement range in battle. It may have been worth shooting at over 200 yards at a large target, such as a close-packed body of men, or where the terrain prevented a closer approach (see the Battle of Homildon Hill, discussed in Chapter Six below). But arrows were expensive and in limited supply, and Mike Loades (2019) is surely correct when he emphasizes the role of point-blank shooting at ranges of 50 yards or less, which would have maximized both the chances of hitting the enemy and the damage that would be done.

Another issue on which Loades makes some valid points is the rate of shooting that could be achieved. He states that he can shoot twelve arrows in a minute with a bow drawing 70 pounds, but that the renowned modern archer Mark Stretton – who shoots with a bow of twice that weight – believes six a minute is more sustainable with heavy bows. In either case, fatigue would quickly reduce these figures, but Loades notes that at these rates even the well-supplied armies of Edward III would soon have run out of arrows. He calculates, for example, that if the English army at the Battle of Crecy (1346) had a million arrows available, at an average rate of eight a minute the roughly 7,500 archers present would have shot them all off in only 16 minutes, leaving themselves defenceless for the rest of the campaign. As far as the percentage of shots that scored a hit is concerned, we have no contemporary figures, but again the well-documented battle at Crecy might provide some indication. According to Froissart (Jolliffe, 1967), the French dead in this catastrophic defeat amounted to about 1,200 men-at-arms and 15,000–16,000 commoners, but by no means all of them were struck by arrows; in fact Froissart, while acknowledging the archers' contribution, implies that it was the English men-at-arms who did most of the work. Even allowing for the chronicler's bias in favour of the deeds of the knightly class, we might not be too far out if we estimate that the archers killed about one Frenchman each, and possibly wounded a few more. And this was when shooting at large bodies of cavalry who were advancing repeatedly to close range. At longer ranges, or against men who were in position to take cover or protect themselves with shields, the proportion of arrows that hit would have been much lower.

The French men-at-arms were well armoured, and many of them would have been struck by arrows which glanced off their armour or otherwise failed to penetrate it. The ability of arrows to penetrate armour has been discussed by several modern writers, with the support of both theoretical physics and experimental results (see for example the appendices in Hardy, 1992, and Strickland & Hardy, 2005; Stretton, 2018; and Loades, 2019). One common conclusion is that no armour could withstand an arrow with an armour-piercing head which was shot under optimum conditions. Mark Stretton (2018) has shot arrows through a reproduction fifteenth-century steel breastplate to a depth which might well have incapacitated anyone wearing it, but he was using a bow of 140 pounds draw weight – well beyond the average archer – at a range of only 15 yards, and even then not all the hits penetrated. Mail would have offered less protection than plate, but when combined with a thick aketon worn underneath it would have provided a fair amount of protection. It is reasonable to conclude that under battlefield conditions, against moving targets at varying ranges and angles, armour was effective enough to justify its weight and expense, even if it was never completely arrow-proof. Loades has argued persuasively that a non-penetrating hit from close range archery could have had an impact similar to that of a punch from a heavyweight boxer, and a series of these would gradually degrade a man's ability to fight. This might have been what happened to the Earl of Douglas at Homildon Hill, who was captured after being struck by at least five arrows. It has been argued recently that the impact of a heavy arrow in the chest area could cause a cardiac arrest, even if the victim's armour was not penetrated. Nevertheless, although perhaps a theoretical possibility, this is not supported by either medieval accounts or modern medical evidence. (See Stretton, 2018, and Loades, 2019. I have discussed this issue at more length in *Clan Battles*, Chapter 3.)

The Scottish Spearmen

As noted in the previous chapter, the Scottish cavalry had never been a match for their English counterparts in numbers, and in the century-and-a-quarter after the Second Battle of Alnwick they too concentrated on the development of the infantry into the decisive arm. However, it evolved in a very different direction from that followed by the English. When a Scottish army defeated the Norwegians at the Battle of Largs in 1263, its infantry were still relying mainly on bows and axes (see my *Highland Battles*, Chapter 8), but before the end of the century their somewhat undisciplined warriors had been transformed into the famous schiltrons, close-packed formations of men drawn up several ranks deep and armed with spears approximately 12–14ft in length (Heath, 1982). These weapons were used not for throwing but to thrust at close quarters, and because of their long reach they were ideally suited to stopping the headlong rush of the English knights, especially when held firmly in both hands. The formation also had its disadvantages, however. The spearmen needed to operate in close order to enable them to support each other, preventing an enemy slipping past the spearpoints and attacking them with swords or other shorter and handier weapons. Therefore, the schiltrons could only manoeuvre at a fairly slow pace and were easily disrupted by terrain obstacles. Furthermore, the troops, being drawn from the common people, could not afford the comprehensive armour protection that the knightly class was accustomed to wearing, and the small shields which they carried had to be slung on their backs when they used both hands to wield their spears. This meant that they were very vulnerable to missiles, a weakness that could be tolerated when their main opponents were the lance-armed knights of the thirteenth century, but which became a serious problem when the English began to increase the number and effectiveness of their bowmen in the fourteenth century.

The long spear was not a new weapon, and neither was the technique of holding it in both hands to thrust. A Pictish warrior is depicted doing just this on the Aberlemno Stone, which is believed to date from the ninth century (see the illustration in Heath, 1980, p.78). The combination of thrusting spear and close fighting order seems to have first appeared in the 1290s in the armies of William Wallace, although it did echo roughly contemporary developments in continental Europe. For example, the newly reorganized Flemish infantry, armed with long spears and polearms, soundly defeated the French cavalry at Courtrai in 1302. The French chronicler Jean de Waurin, writing of Flemish pikemen in the 1470s, tells us that a pike thrust in the chest was invariably fatal to a horse, while in the case of the riders 'nor is there any armour, however good, that [the pikes] cannot pierce or break' (Woosnam-Savage, 2017). (A pike in this context is simply a longer version of the spear; there is no precise definition of how long a spear has to be before it becomes a pike, but conventionally the 12ft spears popular in the fourteenth century are contrasted with the 18ft pikes introduced towards the end of the fifteenth century.) The success of such weapons against armour is understandable because the design of the pike meant that the whole weight of the head and the wooden shaft was concentrated in single sharp point, in contrast to a blow with an edged weapon, whose force, however great, was spread along the length of the edge in contact. Apart from the tactical advantages of these weapons, a move towards infantry spearmen had universal appeal on economic grounds, a lightly equipped infantryman being far cheaper to recruit and equip than a fully armoured nobleman on a specially bred and trained horse. This was particularly relevant in places like Scotland, where suitable land for raising these big horses was in short supply. At first, however, Scottish commanders seem to have been uncertain how best to deploy their schiltrons. At Stirling Bridge in 1297, the English played into Wallace's hands by trying to force their way across a narrow bridge over the River Forth, and the Scots descended on the enemy vanguard before the rest of their army could cross to support them. The result was that the English had no room to deploy properly and were crushed between the spears and the river. In the following year at Falkirk, however, Wallace drew up his men in a defensive position in four circular schiltrons protected by barricades made of stakes and ropes, with archers stationed in between them. The problem was that this deprived the spearmen of their ability to manoeuvre, meaning they were unable to assist their archers when the English knights rode them down, bypassing the massed spears and then attacking them from the rear. Even this manoeuvre was not decisive because the sides of the schiltrons could face outwards and defend themselves from all directions, but when King Edward came up with the main English army he quickly realized the futility of trying to charge the spearmen, so he deployed his own archers and shot down the Scots where they stood.

Despite the new predominance of close-order spear-fighting tactics, the axe remained popular with Scottish troops, and Froissart (Jolliffe, 1967), writing at the end of the fourteenth century, mentions axes on several occasions as still being a characteristic Scottish weapon. He says that the Scots 'are not skilled in archery, but they all carry battle-axes over their shoulders with which they deal fearsome blows in battle'. Froissart also tells us that Scottish armies were far more mobile than the English because most of them rode small ponies on campaign, even though they dismounted to fight, and they did not take cumbersome baggage trains with them but lived off the land and what they could steal. Even cooking pots were unnecessary, because the soldiers were accustomed to frugal living at home and could survive on oat cakes cooked on hot stones and beef boiled in the hides of the slaughtered cattle.

Bannockburn and the Scottish Ascendancy

The decisive battle of the Scottish Wars of Independence against England took place in 1314 at Bannockburn, near Stirling, where Robert the Bruce's spearmen were pitted against Edward II's knights, who were poorly supported on this occasion by archers. A great deal has been written about this battle and many details are still controversial, but from a tactical point of view the general course of events is fairly clear. After the capture of Berwick in 1296, Edward I had gone on to take control of most of Scotland in the name of his puppet king, John Balliol. This was despite the heroic resistance of the Scots under the leadership of William Wallace. Wallace was captured and executed in 1305, but a year later another Scottish leader had emerged in the person of Robert the Bruce, a distant descendant of David I, who was crowned King of Scots in March 1306. Robert initially faced strong opposition from rival factions within Scotland, and after he was defeated by an English cavalry charge at Methven in June 1306 he was forced to go into hiding. However, he then staged a remarkable comeback, thwarting the English knights at the Battle of Loudoun Hill by deploying his spearmen on the defensive behind rows of ditches. He went on to eliminate his rivals at home in a series of campaigns over the next few years. In this he was undoubtedly helped by the fact that Edward I died in 1307 and his successor, Edward II, was much less successful as a war leader and was distracted by continual unrest in England. By 1313, Bruce had not only secured his position among the Scots but had recaptured most of the castles which had been occupied by the English. Of those that remained, the most important was at Stirling, which controlled the crossing of the River Forth and thus the main line of communication between the northern and southern halves of the realm. When Robert's brother, Edward, forced the garrison to agree to surrender if it was not relieved by Midsummer Day 1314, the English king had no choice but to lead an army north to intervene. As many as 26,000 foot-soldiers were called up, but we do not know how many actually joined the army, and it has been estimated that Edward had only around 11,000 infantry and 2,000 cavalry available to fight when he met King Robert at Bannockburn on 23 June (Strickland & Hardy, 2005).

The Scottish army included contingents from many of the kingdom's Highland clans – notably the MacDonalds – as well as the Lowland spearmen and about 500 horsemen, but it was still only about half the size of Edward's force. Bruce nevertheless managed to counter every move that his opponents made. On the first day of the battle, Edward's heavily armoured knights attacked the schiltrons without infantry support and were pushed back in disorder. Bruce may have intended to break off the engagement that night, but he was informed by a deserter that the morale of the English was low and that they were camped in a marshy area where any retreat would be difficult, so he decided to take the offensive on the following day. When battle was joined again on the 24th, the English archers advanced on the right wing, but were ridden down by the Scottish cavalry, while Edward's knights once again failed to make any impression on the close-packed schiltrons. The battlefield was too narrow for a wide outflanking move which might have allowed the English cavalry to break the deadlock, and many of them seem to have been stuck in the rear, unable to get far enough forward to influence the fight. At this point Bruce led the Highlanders against the English flank, and his victory was assured when a body of Scottish camp followers and servants were seen approaching the field. The English soldiers mistook them for enemy reinforcements and a panic broke out. Many of the English were trapped in the marshes and killed, or drowned while trying to cross the Forth. Others took refuge in Bothwell Castle in Lanarkshire and were captured when it surrendered, although Edward himself escaped. Stirling Castle also fell to the Scots, who destroyed it to prevent it being recaptured. By the end of 1315, only Berwick was still in English hands, and that town finally fell three years later (see Chapter Three).

For several years after their victory at Bannockburn, Scottish armies maintained their ascendancy over the English. The Battle of Myton-on-Swale was one of their early successes when taking the offensive into England. It was fought in North Yorkshire in October 1319, between a Scottish raiding army under James Douglas – who had fought with distinction at Bannockburn – and a hastily raised English force led by the Archbishop and Mayor of York. The near-contemporary collection of Norman French chronicles known as *The Brut* (Brie, 1906) describes the local English levies as 'husbandmen that knew nothing of war', and they were accompanied by a large number of monks, priests and friars who were no doubt equally lacking in military expertise. They crossed the River Swale, only to be counterattacked and driven back into the river by the Scots, who charged under the cover of smoke from burning haystacks. Various sources give the English casualties as between 1,000 and 5,000. Further vindication of the Scots' tactics came three years later, paradoxically in an encounter fought between two English forces. The Battle of Boroughbridge was fought in March 1322, only 3 miles from Myton on the River Are. It saw an army under the Earl of Lancaster, who was in revolt against Edward II, pitted against a force of levies from the Borders led by Sir Andrew de Harclay. Having evidently learned from his northern enemies, Harclay deployed a force of infantry armed with long spears 'after the Scottish fashion', as Richard of Durham specifically tells us, but also well supported by archers. Lancaster tried to force his way across the river with his mounted knights, who were spitted on the spears as their predecessors had been at Bannockburn. One of their commanders, Sir Roger de Clifford, had lost his father in just this way in 1314, and was himself wounded and captured at Boroughbridge by fellow Englishmen using the same tactics. Harclay was made Earl of Carlisle for his victory, and might have gone on to further develop this effective fusion of Scottish schiltrons and English archery, but a year later he was hanged, drawn and quartered for treason, having taken it upon himself to make a treaty with the Scots without the consent of the king.

With the innovative Harclay removed from the scene, the run of Scottish victories continued for almost another decade. In August 1322, Edward II led a full-scale invasion in retaliation for Robert the Bruce's support of Lancaster's rebellion, but the Scots implemented their habitual scorched earth policy and withdrew their forces north of the River Forth. Sickness and hunger soon forced the English to withdraw, and Bruce followed them back south in what became known as the 'Great Raid', leading an army which included many Highlanders recruited from Argyll and the Isles. As the Scots approached Rievaulx Abbey in Yorkshire, where King Edward was staying, a loyalist army under the Earl of Richmond deployed to stop them near Byland Abbey. Richmond's position appeared to be a strong one as both his flanks were protected by steep hills, but in the subsequent Battle of Old Byland, Bruce pinned the English with a frontal attack, while his Highlanders – 'Irschery', or Irish, as Barbour describes them, perhaps implying that they were equipped differently from the bulk of the Scots – climbed the slopes and charged downhill into their rear. Sir Thomas Grey, whose father fought in this campaign, described the panic-stricken English fleeing from the Scots 'as a hare before greyhounds' (King, 2005). Edward himself was forced to make a hasty retreat from Rievaulx, leaving his luggage behind.

In January 1327, Edward was overthrown by a rebellion led by his queen, Isabella, and her lover, Roger Mortimer. He was imprisoned and forced to abdicate, and on 1 February his 14-year-old son was crowned as King Edward III, with his mother and Mortimer serving as regents. Mortimer was now in de facto control of the government of England, and in July he led an army north for another campaign against the Scots. Froissart says that this was in response to a challenge issued by Robert the Bruce, who saw the change of monarch as an opportunity to further weaken England, threatening to ravage the northern counties as he had done after Bannockburn if young Edward refused to meet him in battle. The English army assembled at York, where it was reinforced by several hundred men-at-arms from the continent, recruited by Sir John of Hainault. Unfortunately, a quarrel broke out between the foreigners and the English archers, which led to hundreds of deaths and a lasting enmity between the two groups. Edward III held his court at York with great ceremony, knighting fifteen new candidates to join the 600 knights who had accompanied him, but this could not disguise the reality that he was commander in name only, the real authority being wielded by Roger Mortimer, who was no better at controlling his nobles than Edward II had been. Meanwhile, the Scots had crossed the border and were burning and pillaging as far south as Durham. King Robert was ill, and in his absence the army was commanded by two of his most trusted nobles – Thomas Randolph, the 1st Earl of Moray, and Sir James Douglas.

The English army set out for Durham at the beginning of July, and when they arrived there on the 15th they could see the smoke from burning villages in the hills to the west. The following day, they marched out to locate the Scottish army. Here, says Froissart, they were on the borders of the 'deserts' of Northumberland. They spent the next two weeks marching and countermarching through the hilly country around Weardale, constantly wet and exhausted and with their food supplies dwindling, but they failed to bring the enemy to battle. Eventually a scout was captured by the Scots, and released with a message for Edward that Moray and Douglas were waiting for him on a hill 9 miles away. On 31 July, the English arrived on the bank of the River Wear near Stanhope Park, County Durham, and found the Scottish army drawn up in battle array in a very strong position on the far side of the river. A frontal attack would have been suicidal, so they camped in an uncomfortable spot on hard, rocky ground, and were kept awake all night by the Scots blowing horns and howling, as Froissart puts it, as if 'all the devils in hell were coming to strangle them'. The two sides faced each other for three days, skirmishing half-heartedly, until the Scots decamped in the middle of the night and took up a position on another hill nearby. The English followed them but still dared not attack, and Moray and Douglas refused all invitations to come down onto level ground, where they could be attacked on more equal terms. This stalemate went on for three weeks, enlivened only by a night raid led by James Douglas, who crossed the river, killed 300 Englishmen and even cut the guy ropes on the king's tent as he withdrew. Finally, the Scots disappeared again by night and marched for the border. The English only discovered their departure when it was far too late to pursue them. It appears from Froissart's account that Mortimer had thought that he was slowly starving the Scots into submission, but the English were astonished by the number of slaughtered cattle in the abandoned camp and the amount of meat which they found left behind in the cauldrons ready to be cooked. Many more cattle had already been driven away to Scotland, with so many crops taken or burnt that large areas of the North later had to be exempted from taxes until they recovered. Mortimer led his demoralized army back to Durham, where John of Hainault's men, who had achieved nothing at all except to kill some of their allies, were paid off at great expense. Even though no battle had actually been lost, the campaign was regarded in England as a humiliating failure, a view which was reinforced when the Scots returned in the autumn, besieged Norham and blockaded an English garrison in Alnwick. No relief army was sent because there was no money to pay for it, although Isabella and Mortimer's increasingly extravagant lifestyle was beginning to attract unfavourable comment. Mortimer's popularity was further damaged in September when the death of the former Edward II was announced. The circumstances are unclear even today, but it was widely rumoured that the regent had him murdered in gruesome fashion.

After the Weardale campaign, Robert the Bruce found himself in an even stronger position than before, and he exploited this to propose terms for a permanent end to the war. In 1328, the Treaty of Edinburgh-Northampton was signed by Bruce and the young King Edward, and ratified by the English Parliament. Edward agreed to recognize Scotland's independence, free of any English claims to sovereignty, and to accept the restoration of the border between the two countries as it had been in the reign of Alexander III, in other words along the line of the Tweed, leaving Berwick in Scottish hands. Edward, however, regarded the treaty as a humiliating defeat for England, and probably never intended to observe its terms. A year after the agreement was signed, King Robert was dead. He was succeeded by his 5-year-old son, David II, but the succession was disputed by Edward Balliol, son of the Bruce's predecessor, John I, who began to gather support from those Scottish nobles who had been disinherited during the wars. Meanwhile, in 1330, Edward III took power into his own hands and had Mortimer executed for treason. While outwardly still adhering to the terms of the treaty, he secretly backed Balliol, and in July 1332 the latter landed in Fife in English ships with an army which was supposedly recruited from Scottish nobles disinherited by the Bruce. It was far from being a popular uprising against the regime, however; according to the writer known as the Canon of Bridlington, it comprised only 500 men-at-arms and 1,000 infantry, many of whom were English archers. But by this time the Bruce's greatest commander, Sir James Douglas, was also dead, having fallen while on crusade against the Muslims of Granada, and command of the Scottish army sent to face Balliol was in the hands of Thomas Randolph, the Earl of Moray, who was acting as regent for David. Moray was an experienced general who had distinguished himself at Bannockburn, but he seems to have been in poor health and he died (or according to rumour was poisoned by the English) before he could bring the invaders to battle. When Balliol arrived, the Scots thus lacked effective overall control, and were still operating in two separate columns which were led respectively by the earls of Mar in the north and March in the south. The invaders' landing at Kinghorn was opposed only by a few local levies, who were unable to stop them getting ashore. According to *The Brut*, Balliol seized a supply base at Dunfermline and captured 500 long spears or pikes, furnished with long iron heads, which the late Earl of Moray had ordered but not lived long enough to distribute. Balliol gave these to the strongest of his men, who seem from the course of the subsequent battle to have been either men-at-arms or infantrymen who were attached to their formations to support them. It has been suggested that the men-at-arms were drawn up three deep, with the spearmen in a fourth rank behind them (Rogers, 2000).

Dupplin Moor

Balliol clearly wished to avoid being trapped between two enemy forces, so he marched north to confront the Earl of Mar, who was deployed on the far bank of the River Earn near Perth. All the sources agree that the Scottish army was by far the stronger, although estimates of its actual numbers vary widely. But Mar seems to have been careless about deploying sentries, and on the night of 11 August the invaders managed to get across the river by an unguarded ford and attacked the Scottish camp. They caused many casualties, but the main body of the Scots remained intact, and on the following morning they deployed into battle formation and counterattacked. The ensuing Battle of Dupplin Moor has always been of great interest to historians, because it has been seen as the genesis of the English tactics which gave them a decisive advantage at Halidon Hill, and subsequently in the first phase of the Hundred Years' War against France. The location of the battlefield is not precisely known, but according to *The Brut* the English were drawn up in a narrow passage where the terrain obliged the Scots to attack on a very restricted front. Balliol dismounted most of his men-at-arms, leaving only about forty on horseback to act as a reserve, and deployed them on a frontage of no more than 200 yards. The archers were placed on the flanks in a formation which became characteristic of Hundred Years' War battles, although on this occasion it is likely that it was adopted because of the narrow frontage available rather than as a deliberate tactical innovation (Strickland & Hardy, 2005, Chapter 11).

The Scottish army advanced in two battles, led by the Earl of Mar and Robert Bruce, an illegitimate son of the late king. *The Brut* claims that Bruce had accused Mar of collusion with the enemy, and that the earl attempted to refute the charge by being the first to attack. Bruce, however, moved first, and the two commands raced each other in increasing disorder towards the English line. It seems certain that the Scots intended to attack on foot with long spears in the schiltron formations that had been so successful at Bannockburn, but for maximum effect this required a steady advance in close order rather than a hasty charge. As Bruce approached Balliol's centre, the English archers began shooting from both sides, and according to the *Lanercost Chronicle* (Maxwell, 1913), many of the Scots were blinded or wounded in their unprotected faces. Nevertheless, their numbers and momentum carried them forward, and at first they pushed the Englishmen back. But then, says the chronicler, one of the English commanders, Lord Stafford, ordered his men to 'turn your shoulders instead of your breasts to the pikes'. No doubt the intention was that by turning side-on to the enemy, they would be able to stand closer together and oppose them with a denser row of their own spear points, and as soon as this was done the Englishmen began to regain the lost ground. Just as Bruce's men were falling back, Mar brought up his division, but instead of bringing it into action alongside their comrades and attacking the archers who were continuing to shoot into their flanks, he simply led them straight forward into Bruce's rear. Here they could achieve nothing useful, and only impeded the movements of their comrades. According to an English eyewitness, Sir Thomas Grey, they knocked many of their own men down even as Balliol's men pushed into them from the opposite direction. At the same time, the Scots were also squeezed from both sides as the men on the flanks tried to get away from the arrows which were still galling them. The stage was now set for one of the worst disasters that could befall a medieval army. The Scottish soldiers in the middle of the crowd were soon so tightly crammed together that they could no longer raise their arms to defend themselves, and were in more danger of being trampled by their own comrades than of being killed by the enemy. Andrew de Wyntoun, whose *Original Chronicle* was written around 1425, says that 'whoever in that great throng fell never had the chance to rise again'. The *Bridlington Chronicle* describes how they fell 'in a great heap', so that many were killed by suffocation, 'whose number no one knows'. The Scottish rear ranks fled and were pursued by the mounted men-at-arms, but there was no escape for the rest. Eventually, the Englishmen surrounded the heap of bodies in the centre and mercilessly slaughtered any who were still alive. Among them was Thomas Randolph's son, Thomas, 2nd Earl of Moray, who had held the earldom for only three weeks. Other Scottish casualties included Robert Bruce, the earls of Mar, Moray and Mentieth, and – according to the Bridlington chronicler – about 2,000 knights and men-at-arms, as well as countless foot-soldiers.

Balliol quickly moved to exploit his unexpected victory and marched to nearby Scone, where the Kings of Scots had traditionally been crowned. On 24 September, he had himself proclaimed king, after which he repaid Edward III for his support by granting him extensive estates in Scotland, among which was included the town of Berwick. But many Scots still supported young David II, and on 16 December Balliol was ambushed at Annan in Dumfriesshire by an army led by Archibald Douglas and John Randolph, who had succeeded his brother, Thomas, as 3rd Earl of Moray. Edward's brother, Henry Balliol, was killed and most of their supporters scattered. Edward himself fled ignominiously to England, where his pleas for help gave his namesake Edward III the pretext which he had been seeking to abandon the Treaty of Edinburgh-Northampton and begin preparations for all-out war. Meanwhile, the Scots were still occupying Berwick and were determined not to give it up.

They reinforced the garrison and prepared for a siege. In March 1333, Balliol arrived with an advanced guard and besieged the town, being joined in early May by King Edward with the main English army. This force included two counterweight trebuchets, the most advanced siege engines of the time, which threw heavy stone missiles that caused considerable damage to the defences. By the end of June, the garrison was running out of supplies and the governor of the town, Sir Alexander Seton, asked Edward for a truce. This was granted on the condition that Berwick would surrender if it was not relieved, and Seton was obliged to give up twelve hostages – including his son, Thomas – as a guarantee that this condition would be observed.

The Scottish relief force had been entrusted to Sir Archibald Douglas, who as Guardian of Scotland was ruling as regent on behalf of David II. A brother of Robert the Bruce's leading supporter, Sir James Douglas, Sir Archibald was the fourth regent to have held office during David's brief reign to date, the first three having been either killed in battle, captured or allegedly poisoned by the English. He seems to have been reluctant to engage the enemy in a pitched battle, but now action was imperative if Berwick was not to be lost. On 11 July, he crossed the Tweed, marched around the besieged town and burnt Tweedmouth, on the south bank of the river, in an unsuccessful attempt to draw Edward away from Berwick. Meanwhile, a force of 200 horsemen under Sir William Keith managed to cross back to the north bank via a damaged bridge and enter the town. Two days later, Douglas sent a message to Edward demanding that he keep to the agreement and leave, as Berwick had now been relieved. The king rejected this demand on the grounds that as Keith had entered surreptitiously from the south, rather than from Scotland, his arrival could not be said to be a relief of the siege. He reinforced his argument by building a gallows within sight of the walls and hanging Thomas Seton from it in sight of his parents, threatening to execute another two hostages every day until Berwick surrendered. Keith then took over the negotiations and persuaded Edward to agree to an extension of the truce until 19 July. Obviously learning from the problems which the vagueness of the previous arrangement had caused, this time the parties set out clear conditions for what was meant by a relief. Douglas had either to get at least 200 men-at-arms into the town, drive the English from the northern shore of the Tweed or defeat them in open battle.

Douglas again tried to force Edward to raise the siege by threatening Bamburgh, where the English queen, Philippa, was in residence, but her husband remained as unmoved by the risk to his wife as he was by thc devastation which the Scots were inflicting on the Northumberland countryside. Instead of abandoning Berwick, he deployed his army on the high ground of Halidon Hill to the north-east of the town, from where he could observe the approaches from all directions. This amounted to a challenge to battle, and with time running out Douglas had little choice but to accept it. He did, however, attempt to improve his chances by some clever strategic manoeuvring. He recrossed the Tweed, passed through the small town of Duns 15 miles north-west of Berwick and advanced towards the English from the north. If he could break into Berwick from this direction, he would leave Edward with no honourable alternative but to abandon the siege, while if he defeated his enemies in a pitched battle, he might be able to trap them against the river and destroy them completely.

Halidon Hill

Foard and Morris, in their fascinating study on *The Archaeology of English Battlefields* (2012), raise legitimate doubts about the traditional location of the ensuing battle. They argue that if the English army was attempting to stop the Scots entering Berwick, it would have been logical to block the Great North Road, and furthermore that one account describes troops as being deployed on the wing nearest the sea, which implies a site much nearer to the coast. Today the A1, the successor to the Great North Road, bypasses Berwick not far from the eastern slopes of Halidon Hill. The exact route taken by the road in the fourteenth century is not known, but it is likely to have passed through or very close to the medieval town which depended on it for access by land. The encounter between the two armies, these authors suggest, would logically have taken place on the low ground outside Berwick, and later tradition might have transferred it to the hill simply because of its prominence in the local landscape. However, this argument is not particularly convincing. The road must have passed through the relatively narrow corridor between the sea and the hills north of Berwick, so both it and the town itself could easily have been kept under observation from Halidon Hill. Similarly, the North Sea is clearly visible from many locations on the hill itself, so it might have seemed logical to refer to a body of men as deployed on the side nearest the sea, even if the actual distance to the shore was a mile or more.

The Battle of Halidon Hill is fairly well served by contemporary sources, probably because the presence of King Edward himself attracted the attention of the chroniclers. It features in Ranulf Higden's *Polychronicon*, which was completed in the 1350s, and in *The Brut*. The *Anonimalle Chronicle*, written at York in the late fourteenth century, includes a continuation of *The Brut* which features an apparently independent account of the battle (Childs & Taylor, 1991). Also useful is the work of the Canon of Bridlington (Myers, ed., 1969), who tells us that the Scots left Duns at dawn on 19 July, and around 9.00 am they were spotted by English scouts approaching Berwick from the north. King Edward left a detachment, which apparently included 500 men-at-arms, to blockade the town, and deployed the bulk of his army on Halidon Hill in the standard three divisions or battles. The English Heritage Battlefield report says that no evidence has been found of any old fields, woods or hedges predating the enclosures of the 1840s. This suggests that the whole area was open rough pasture in the Middle Ages, though both place name evidence and the statement of Andrew of Wyntoun tell us that the flat ground between the hill and its neighbour to the north-east, Witches' Knowe, was boggy. Edward took command of the centre division himself, with the Earl of Norfolk on the right, 'next to the sea', and Edward Balliol leading the division on the left. Because he needed to prevent the Scots from getting around his army and entering Berwick, the king 'carefully chose out horsemen who would fight together', and presumably deployed these as a reserve towards the rear. The rest of the English fought on foot, with archers 'assigned to each wing'. *The Brut* explains that each battle had two such wings of archers, which must mean that units of bowmen and men-at-arms alternated along the line, rather than the missile troops being deployed on the wings of the entire army – as they had been at Dupplin Moor – or as a line of skirmishers in front. This has often been regarded as the first appearance of what would become the standard deployment of English armies in the Hundred Years' War, with 'wedges' of archers protruding forward from the line held by the men-at-arms so that they could enfilade an enemy seeking to close with them (Strickland & Hardy, 2005). However, we are not specifically told that such wedges were employed at Halidon Hill, and Jim Bradbury (1985) has argued that it is also difficult to find evidence of their use in subsequent battles. For example, Froissart's account of the Battle of Crecy in 1346 has archers drawn up in front of the Prince of Wales's division, and the French knights are described as riding past them (perhaps while making a flank attack?), and later on as breaking through them, in order to engage the men-at-arms. Interspersing archers and men-at-arms may have been a tactic designed by Edward or his advisors specifically for the situation at Halidon, where the curve of the hill would have prevented men stationed on the far wings of the army from seeing what was happening in the centre or shooting at an enemy attacking there. Nevertheless, it was extremely successful on this occasion, which makes it likely that its use was at least considered elsewhere.

As the Scots reached the summit of Witches' Knowe, Douglas seems to have taken note of the English deployment and similarly decided to dismount his own men-at-arms, sending the horses away to the far side of the hill for safety. Both the need to relieve Berwick and the enemy's superiority in missile troops obliged him to take the offensive and close with the English as quickly as possible, but the decision to dismount was probably influenced by the need for the heavily armoured men-at-arms to stiffen the lightly equipped Scots spearmen, and by the rough and boggy nature of the intervening ground, which would have been very difficult going for charging cavalry. The sources disagree about the details of the Scottish deployment, with the Canon of Bridlington and the *Polychronicon* among others describing the usual three divisions, while *The Brut* and the *Anonimalle Chronicle* mention four. Childs and Taylor (1991) point out that the latter two sources give the longest lists of the Scottish noblemen at the battle, including individuals not named elsewhere. This, they argue, suggests that the mention of four divisions is not merely a mistake due to English witnesses observing the army from the far side of the field, but rather that other writers, accustomed to the more traditional arrangement in three bodies or 'battles', have omitted the extra division and its leaders from their orders of battle. Whatever the case, Archibald Douglas placed his own division on the left, because it was there that a breakthrough was most urgent in order to reach Berwick and lift the siege. The right-hand division was under the command of the Earl of Moray, the third John Randolph. According to the *Chronica de Melsa*, the Scots were ordered to wear white shirts over their armour so that they could be easily distinguished from the enemy. The *Anonimalle Chronicle* tells us that the English were 'very cast down' when they saw the size of the host in front of them, but that the king rode among them and encouraged them, promising rewards to those who fought well. On the other side, says the Canon of Bridlington, Douglas was similarly haranguing his soldiers, explaining that the enemy were in effect already prisoners, as they were hemmed in on four sides between his advancing army, the sea, the River Tweed and the town of Berwick, still held by its Scottish garrison.

We have no reliable information on the total strengths of the two armies. The *Lanercost Chronicle* says that the English numbered 30,000 and were outnumbered two-to-one, while the *Chronicon de Melsa* puts the odds at three-to-one, which would give the Scots an implausible total of 90,000 men. The *Chronicle of Walter of Guisborough* (also known as Walter of Hemingburgh), however, gives a detailed account of the Scottish order of battle which is greatly at variance with every other writer, but seems altogether more realistic, if suspiciously precise (Rothwell, 1957). According to this source, the first division (presumably that led by Douglas) comprised 300 men-at-arms and 2,200 more lightly equipped commoners; the second division eleven knights, 300 men-at-arms and 3,000 infantry; the third division seventeen knights, 300 men -at-arms and 4,400 infantry; and the fourth division twelve knights, 200 men-at-arms and 4,000 footmen. This adds up to 14,740 men, so if Edward's men were indeed outnumbered by about two-to-one they would therefore have been between 7,000 and 8,000 strong. The role played by the Highland contingent in this battle is unclear, but as none of our sources mention them specifically, it seems unlikely that they operated separately from the main schiltrons. Sixteenth-century writers such as John Major were insistent that Highlanders were armed differently from the bulk of the Scottish troops, and what accounts we have of the battles between the clans in the fifteenth century confirm that they were fought by men armed mainly with bows and axes who relied heavily on mobility, discharging a volley of missiles before charging rapidly into hand-to-hand combat (see my *Clan Battles* volume). This does not seem to be compatible with the sort of steady advance in close order with long spears described in accounts of battles such as Bannockburn, but although the contribution of Bruce's Highlanders in that encounter was crucial, no account suggests that this was because they fought differently from their Lowland compatriots. However, it seems from accounts of the Battle of Flodden (1513) that, at least on some occasions, Highlanders serving in a Scottish national army did continue to have a separate tactical function, just as they had done under Bruce at Old Byland. For example, Robert Lindesay of Pitscottie contrasts the disaster which befell James IV's pike-armed centre at Flodden with the exploits of the Earl of Huntly's Highlanders. The same author later divides the army of James V into two equal parts, with 20,000 'in jak and speir' and 20,000 – presumably the Highlanders – bearing 'haberjouns and tua handit suordis'. Whether this distinction applied in fourteenth-century armies, however, we do not know. It would seem unlikely that the Highlanders would have been obliged to give up the traditional weapons with which they were already skilled in order to fight in the Lowland style, or that this could have been enforced, even if their commanders had wished it and had a supply of long spears ready to issue. Tomb effigies of West Highland chiefs from this period often depict men armed with jack (a fabric jacket reinforced with iron plates), spear, shield and sword. Such men would have been fully compliant with Robert the Bruce's 1318 Statute of Arms, and would surely have been capable of taking their places in the schiltrons (Heath, 1982). That is probably what they did, unless a particular tactical situation called for their special skills to be employed in a different role, as may have happened at Old Byland. For example, Earl Hugh of Ross (or Aodh in Gaelic), who appears to have fought in Douglas's division at Halidon Hill, was surely a quintessential Highlander, in so far as the distinction can be made in the fourteenth century: he was the great-great grandson of Farquhar MacTaggart, who had been awarded the earldom for his services to King Alexander II against the MacHeth and MacWilliam rebels in 1215 (see my *Highland Battles*, Chapter 6).

Despite their apparent advantage in numbers, the Scots did not attack at once. According to the *Anonimalle Chronicle*, they waited until midday before they came down from Witches' Knowe and advanced towards the English line. The chronicler says that they delayed until the tide at the mouth of the River Tweed was high enough to prevent the English from retreating. In the meantime, according to Geoffrey le Baker, a Scottish champion named William Turnbull went out into no-man's land, accompanied by an enormous mastiff, and challenged any Englishman to fight him. This Turnbull was originally named Roull, but was said to have earned his new appellation when out hunting with Robert the Bruce in Perthshire. The king had been unexpectedly charged by a wild bull, and Roull had saved his life by seizing the animal by the horns and throwing it to the ground. Whether true or not, the story implies that Turnbull was known as a man of great strength, but nevertheless Sir Robert Benhale of Norfolk accepted the challenge. The two men met halfway between the two armies, in full view of both sides. Although he was much smaller in stature than his opponent, the younger and more agile Benhale killed first the dog and then its owner, returning to the army with Turnbull's severed head. Robson (1897) quotes the seventeenth-century English historian, Joshua Barnes, who gives a blow-by-blow account of the encounter which, as Robson says, should be accepted 'with considerable reserve', but just might incorporate a genuine memory of a fight which must have been witnessed by several thousand people:

> 'He (Turnbull) strake at him with all his might. Sir Robert suddenly eludes the blow, and while the adversary, bending down his right side and rearing at the same time his left arm, was recovering his overpoised body, in that very instant Benhale steps boldly in, and with one home blow divides his left arm from his body.'

Even this did not immediately fell the Scot, who even as he bled to death continued to strike at his enemy, but Benhale avoided every attack and eventually 'with one blow cuts off Turnbull's head'.

Undeterred by this omen, the Scottish army then marched forward to attack. The Earl of Moray's division on the right had the shortest distance to cover and was the first into action, but the march across the boggy ground slowed and disorganized them, and at the end of it they had to climb a short but steep slope to close with the enemy drawn up along the top. Andrew of Wyntoun explains that the Scots had not given proper consideration to the nature of the ground, and that – although this was not obvious from a distance – the slope of Halidon Hill proved so steep that one man standing on the top could easily hold off three attackers. This feature can still be clearly seen today, and it can be appreciated how it helped the English defence by forcing the Scots to slow down at the most dangerous point of their advance, when they were exposed to arrows shot with full power from a range of between 10 and 20 yards. This would have been exactly the sort of decisive close range shooting that Mike Loades (see above, 'The English Bowmen', p.46) considers to be the true role of the longbow. Moray's men were especially eager to defeat Balliol, whom they considered to be a traitor, but the *Lanercost Chronicle* tells us that so many of them were wounded in the face or blinded by arrows as they turned their unprotected faces up towards their opponents on the higher ground, that they were forced to fall back even before the other Scottish divisions could enter the fight. Those who tried to close with King Edward's own battle fared no better, and were similarly brought to a halt by a combination of the terrain and English archery.

On the Scottish left, however, where their best troops were deployed, the fight was much fiercer. From Walter of Guisborough's order of battle, it appears that the proportion of armoured men-at-arms to unprotected spearmen was much higher in this decisive sector. The Canon of Bridlington says that they charged with the ferocity of lions, desperate to break through to Berwick, while the English resisted with equal determination, with the fight lasting for most of the day. This must surely mean that here at least the Scots succeeded in getting close enough for hand-to-hand combat. Eventually, through 'divine providence', the English got the upper hand. *The Brut* says that the Scottish commanders had to rally their battered companies several times before they were finally forced to fall back, leaving 500 of their best men dead on the field, including Archibald Douglas himself. This part of the hill, the Canon adds, was later known as 'Hevyside' on account of the slaughter. Wyntoun singles out Hugh, the Earl of Ross, for special praise because of the protracted resistance which he mounted, but adds that his bravery was of little use because he and all his men were eventually killed. The Scots then turned in flight, but the men-at-arms, already hampered by their heavy armour, found to their dismay that their horses were no longer where they had left them. According to *The Brut*, when the squires who had been left in charge of the animals saw their masters getting the worst of the fight, they took the horses and rode off to safety, leaving their owners to be overtaken and slaughtered. The English mounts had evidently been kept close behind the lines, because the same source adds that Edward's knights rode after the fleeing enemy for 7 leagues, which would have taken them well past Duns and into the hills of the Southern Uplands. As William Patten pointed out in his account of the English pursuit after the Battle of Pinkie (1547), mounted pursuers were unable to reach low enough to strike at the bodies of opponents on foot, so most of their blows landed on heads and necks, and a very high proportion of them were consequently fatal. According to the *Lanercost Chronicle*, the English struck down their opponents with iron maces, a remark which – if not merely a figure of speech – suggests they were specially equipped with weapons designed to inflict concussive blows on men wearing armour and helmets. The chroniclers' tallies of Scottish dead are clearly as exaggerated as their estimates of the original army, but they do give an impression of an overwhelming disaster. Geoffrey le Baker says 60,000 died, the *Anonimalle Chronicle* 40,000 and *The Brut* a suspiciously precise 35,712. The Canon of Bridlington says that among them were seven earls, twenty-five baronets and forty-seven ordinary knights. The earls included those of Ross, Lennox, Sutherland, Carrick, Menteith and Athol; the seventh was presumably Archibald Douglas, though the earldom was actually established for his son, William, who was officially the 1st Earl of Douglas. Reported English losses were insignificant, with only one knight and thirteen others killed according to the *Chronica de Melsa*, although if the Canon of Bridlington is correct about the prolonged fight on the Scottish left this must surely be a gross underestimate.

The generally accepted location of the Battle of Halidon Hill is within easy walking distance of Berwick-upon-Tweed. From the railway station, follow the A6105 towards Foulden and Duns. After about half a mile, you will have to cross the A1, but there is seldom enough traffic on it to make this a problem. After another 300 yards, take the first road on the right, ascending a hill with a prominent radio tower on the top. Near the crest is a car park, and just beyond, next to the tower, is one of a series of interpretation boards with a map showing a network of trails that criss-cross the battlefield. Following these, it is possible to explore the site as far as Witches' Knowe, 2 miles to the north west.

Chapter Five

'Without Cowardice or Faint Hearts': Otterburn, 1388

Date	5 August 1388
Location	Near Otterburn, Redesdale, Northumberland
Combatants	Scots under James, 2nd Earl of Douglas, versus English led by Sir Henry Percy, 'Hotspur'
Outcome	Scottish victory

IN THE AFTERMATH of the defeat at Halidon Hill, the 9-year-old King David fled to France, where King Philip VI welcomed him and installed him in state at Chateau Gaillard. Meanwhile, Edward Balliol repaid Edward III for his support by ceding Lothian to England while he attempted to make his claim to the rest of the Scottish kingdom a reality, but in 1335 he was defeated by David's supporters at the Battle of Culblean. Over the next few years, the loyalists gradually expelled the English from their strongholds in Scotland. Edinburgh was recaptured in 1341, and the now 17-year-old king returned in triumph. In June 1346, when he learned that Edward was planning an invasion of France, Philip VI sent an urgent message to Scotland asking for help. David readily agreed to assist his former host, but mustering an army large enough to invade England was a slow process, and it was not until the beginning of October that he crossed into Cumberland at the head of an estimated 12,000 men, of whom Bower says that 2,000 were very well armoured – perhaps, as Strickland and Hardy suggest, in equipment supplied by the French. According to Geoffrey le Baker, the army included a contingent of Genoese mercenaries, also sent by Philip, who were presumably crossbowmen like their compatriots at the

Battle of Crecy, which was fought between Edward III and a French army on 26 August. Edward had won a decisive victory at Crecy, and by this time was laying siege to Calais. It is not clear whether David was aware of the fact, but the north of England had not been left as defenceless as Philip had led him to believe. Edward had exempted the northern counties when recruiting the army for France, so the Archbishop of York, William de la Zouche, was quickly able to raise an army at Richmond from the men of Northumberland, Cumberland, Yorkshire and Lancashire. Bypassing Carlisle, the Scots crossed the Pennines, sacked Hexham and then moved on towards Durham, where de la Zouche, together with Ralph de Neville and Henry Percy, intercepted them on 17 October at Neville's Cross, just west of the city.

The Battle of Neville's Cross

Although it took place beyond the borders of Northumberland, this battle is worth examining here for the light which it can shed on the evolution of tactics as well as for its long-term significance. The sources do not give a clear picture of events, but it appears that David at first attempted to deploy on the defensive, perhaps recalling the failure of the offensive at Halidon Hill. Then 500 English archers ran forward and shot at the Scots from close range while they were forming up. Wyntoun and Bower say that Sir John Graham, the Earl of Mentieth, then suggested to David that he should take 100 horsemen and drive off the archers, as Sir Robert Keith had done at Bannockburn. But either the king refused to risk his cavalry or, in Bower's version, Graham could find no volunteers and so charged the English alone, but his horse was shot and he was forced to retreat to his own lines on foot. The schiltrons then advanced to the attack. However, on this occasion the effect of the English archery seems to have been limited, probably, as Strickland and Hardy suggest, because the Scots who were wearing French armour had been placed in the front ranks. The same authors quote from a letter written by an English eyewitness, Thomas Samson, who says that de la Zouche's archers and 'common soldiers' were twice forced to retreat, but the men-at-arms stood firm and held the enemy until the bowmen could rally. The latter then moved out onto the flanks of the Scottish spearmen and shot with greater success at their less well protected rear ranks. The right-hand Scottish division, under the Earl of Moray, was eventually pushed back, leaving David's own division in the centre to be enveloped on both flanks. The close-packed spearmen were then forced together into a crush similar to that at Dupplin Moor (see above, Chapter Four). They fought determinedly but finally broke, and David was captured in the rout. Meanwhile, the Scottish left-hand division, led by the Earl of March and Robert Stewart, High Steward of Scotland, had taken no part in the fighting and marched away northwards upon seeing the defeat of the other two divisions, leaving their king to his fate.

Robert was the son of Walter Stewart, the previous High Steward, and Robert the Bruce's daughter, Marjorie. He was thus David's nephew, and his heir if he should die childless, although he was actually older than the king. Later, he was to lead an unsuccessful rebellion against David, which adds credibility to the suspicion that his conduct at Neville's Cross was due to disloyalty rather than caution, but his reputation for loyalty somehow survived, and he was appointed guardian of the kingdom by Parliament in the absence of the king. David remained in prison in various English castles for eleven years. He was only released in 1357 when, by the Treaty of Berwick-upon-Tweed, the Scottish nobility agreed to pay a ransom of 1,000 marks a year for ten years. After six years he stopped paying the ransom, pleading poverty, but managed to avoid retaliation by Edward by dragging out the negotiations until he died in 1371. David was 46 years old, and although he had married twice he had no children. The throne therefore went to his nephew, Robert Stewart. King Robert II, the first of the Stewart (later spelled Stuart) dynasty, was already 56 years old and no match for Edward III. He was not keen on military affairs and lacked the charismatic personality that would have been needed to mobilize his nobles to follow him into battle. Froissart describes his unprepossessing appearance, with 'red, bleary eyes, the colour of sandalwood, which showed that he was no valiant fighter'. He was more interested in consolidating his authority in the north of his kingdom than in war with England, but in pursuit of this objective he inadvertently managed to elevate two local magnates into virtually autonomous rivals. The first of these was John MacDonald, the self-styled Lord of the Isles, who married Robert's daughter and was confirmed in possession of all the extensive lands which he had inherited in the west of Scotland. This was the foundation of the power of the subsequent Lords of the Isles, who were often a thorn in the side of later kings. Meanwhile, on the other side of the country, Robert's illegitimate son, Alexander Stewart, was granted the Lordship of Badenoch and the role of Lieutenant of the North, making him in effect the king's viceroy in the northern half of the country. Alexander's subsequent career of banditry and blackmail earned him the nickname of the 'Wolf of Badenoch' and permanently tarnished the reputation of the Highland 'caterans' whom he employed as his enforcers. The division of Scotland into Highlanders and Lowlanders, amounting at times to mutual hatred, can largely be traced to these developments during the reign of Robert II.

Nevertheless, Robert did succeed in putting the country on a firmer financial footing, partly by increasing the revenue raised from the North, however unreliable his lieutenants may have been, and partly by encouraging the wool trade. Then he gradually increased the pressure on the English, attacking the last garrisons on the Scottish side of the border, at Jedburgh, Roxburgh and Lochmaben. Edward III died in 1377 and was succeeded by his 10-year-old grandson, Richard II. The new king nominally ruled through a council of nobles headed by Sir Simon de Burley and the Earl of Oxford, Robert de Vere, but was strongly under the influence of his uncle, John of Gaunt. John was a supporter of Edward III's aggressive policy towards France, and in the early years of Richard's reign several unsuccessful invasions of the continent took place, requiring increased taxation to pay for them and finally provoking the Peasants' Revolt of 1381. What was worse from the English point of view, the attacks encouraged the French to revive and strengthen their alliance with Scotland. Taking advantage of the political confusion in England, the Scots captured Lochmaben Castle early in 1384 and destroyed it.

Military Developments in the Later Fourteenth Century

By the end of 1384 it was becoming obvious to Richard that the French and the Scots were working together against him, and that it would be necessary to strike soon against one or the other. In May of that year, a small French force under the Admiral of France, Jean de Vienne, had landed in Scotland; it numbered only about 2,000 men, but de Vienne brought with him 50,000 French livres in cash and another 200 suits of armour to help equip the Scottish forces. Froissart says that the Scottish knights were delighted with this equipment, which was much better than their own. The armour of the knightly class at least had been revolutionized in the five decades since Halidon Hill. At the beginning of Edward III's reign, they had essentially worn the same kind of mail protection as their predecessors at Alnwick in 1174. Helmets were now fully enclosed, usually furnished with a visor which protected the face against arrows and could be raised (at some personal risk) for improved visibility or communication. Various items of steel plate were added to protect the limbs, and by the thirteenth century coats of plates, consisting of small metal or whalebone plates riveted to the inside of a leather jacket, were being worn over the mail. But the ultimate goal of the armourer, to enclose the body in a rigid shell of steel, had to wait until developments in metallurgy made possible the production of large pieces which were shaped to fit the wearer's body. Although still very expensive, the manufacture of plate armour was if anything less labour intensive than that of mail (according to Woosnam-Savage, an armourer could produce two suits of plate armour in about three months, compared to the similar time needed to make one mail hauberk), which helped to make it more accessible once the technological difficulties had been overcome. It is not possible to establish an exact date for this development, because few datable pieces of medieval armour of any type survive, and illustrations and tomb effigies generally show armour which was covered with fabric or worn under a surcoat, making it difficult to tell how it was constructed. However, most authorities concur that the first full breastplates appeared round the middle of the fourteenth century, and that soon afterwards older types of protection became superfluous and began to fall out of use. Shields are no longer depicted on English tomb effigies after about 1360 (Heath, 1982), and by the end of the century mail was used mainly to fill in gaps between the plates where extra flexibility was needed, rather than being the first line of defence itself. So it seems likely that the armour which the Scottish knights received from the French would have consisted of up-to-date items such as steel cuirasses, gauntlets and cuisses, or plates to protect the thighs. By 1400, illustrations often show men wearing their plate armour uncovered, a style which was known in French as '*harnois blanc*', or 'white harness', and probably stemmed from the desire of the nobility to show off their expensive new equipment. Similar armour was also widely used in England by this time. Inevitably, the common soldiers of both sides would have to make do with older and cheaper forms of protection for many years to come, but steel breastplates and other items gradually began to percolate down the social scale, aided by the fact that it was much cheaper to repair old second-hand pieces than to forge new ones, until by the mid-fifteenth century even archers are frequently depicted in art wearing items of plate (Heath).

By the 1380s, King Robert had lost much of his authority and his son, John, Earl of Carrick, who was an advocate of a strong anti-English policy, was acting as lieutenant of the kingdom south of the River Forth. It was not in the interests of some of the magnates in the English border regions to maintain the peace either. Rose (2002) points out that Henry Percy, who had been created Earl of Northumberland in 1377, made a substantial fortune out of the wardenship of the Marches. The £1,000 a year that the Crown was spending on border defence at that time increased to £16,000 with the outbreak of war eight years later, and most of that money went to pay Percy to maintain garrisons which in peacetime he would have had to pay for out of his own revenues. To attack both his enemies simultaneously was beyond Richard's capabilities on financial grounds alone, but in June 1385 he decided, or was persuaded, to mount a full-scale invasion of Scotland. This has become famous as the last time that the English feudal levy was ever summoned for war. Technically, the Statute of Winchester of 1285 was still in effect, but it had long ago ceased to be used as the main means of raising English armies. By the middle of the fourteenth century, most troops were raised by means of indentures, which were written contracts between the king and his nobles by which the latter agreed to provide armed retinues of a specified strength (Heath, 1982). The men themselves were in effect paid professionals, recruited from the noblemen's own household retainers or employed via sub-contractors, who often led their men as captains on campaign. This arrangement released the magnates from the unpredictable demands of feudal service, while providing the king with an army of trained and experienced men, who although they were often recruited for a specified period – just as under the feudal system – tended to serve for longer periods and to be prepared to re-enlist if required. The indentured retinues usually consisted of either men-at-arms or archers, with the proportion of the latter increasing over time from about one-to-one in the 1340s to three-to-one by the fifteenth century. By contrast, the Kings of Scots retained an older system known as 'Scottish service', according to which all free men between the ages of 16 and 60 were obliged to muster at eight days' notice and serve for forty days. Indentured retinues on the English model did appear in Scotland around this time (Heath, 1982), but the majority of the ordinary men who made up the schiltrons continued to be recruited on a part-time basis until the end of our period.

Looking south across the River Tweed near Coldstream. Earlier versions of the Ordnance Survey Landranger map located the site of the Battle of Carham here, on the far (English) bank. No reason is given for the choice of this precise location, which no longer appears on the latest edition of the map. This does look like a feasible place for the Scottish army to have forded the river, but in fact its course has changed significantly over the last thousand years.

The 'Lion Bridge' over the River Aln at Alnwick. The present structure dates from the eighteenth century, but the original bridge, which may have been a few yards downstream, was a principal Scottish objective in Malcolm III's campaign of 1093.

The ramparts of Alnwick Castle overlook the valley of the Aln a short distance downstream of the bridge. The extensive curtain walls are fourteenth century. Before it was purchased and rebuilt by the Percy family in 1309, the castle was probably a conventional Norman motte and bailey construction.

A view west along the road leading from Denwick, north of Alnwick. It was at approximately this point that on 13 November 1093, Robert de Mowbray's Anglo-Norman cavalry emerged from a wood and found themselves on the flank of Malcolm Canmore's Scottish army.

The Malcolm Cross near Alnwick marks the spot where Malcolm is thought to have received his fatal wound.

A quarter of a mile down the hill from the Malcolm Cross, next to the road, are the remains of Saint Leonard's Hospital. The hospital was built later on the site of the spring where King Malcolm died.

The memorial on Ratten Row on the outskirts of Alnwick, erected to commemorate the English victory in the Second Battle of Alnwick. The inscription reads, 'William the Lion King of Scotland, besieging Alnwick Castle, was here taken prisoner, 1174'.

The town of Berwick-upon-Tweed, looking south-eastwards from the slopes of Halidon Hill.

Above left: The ruins of Berwick Castle, overlooking the River Tweed at the north end of the town. The first fortifications here were probably built by the Scottish King David I in the twelfth century.

Above right: The radio tower on Halidon Hill, a few yards north of the car park, is a prominent local landmark.

Looking north-west from the English positions on Halidon Hill towards the initial Scottish position on Witches' Knowe. The Scottish schiltrons advanced across the intervening low ground, which in 1333 was undrained and boggy. The structures in the fields in the middle distance house free-range pigs.

This is the view that the advancing Scots would have had as they closed on the English line on Halidon Hill. It is evident that the slope up which they had to advance is steeper than it appears to be when viewed from higher ground.

The board next to the radio tower on Halidon Hill includes a detailed map showing the network of trails that allow access to the battlefield.

The tidal lower reaches of the River Tweed, looking upstream from near the ruins of Berwick Castle. The lower slopes of Halidon Hill are to the right. Edward III's army would have had to escape across this dangerous stretch of water if it had been defeated in the battle.

The battlefield of Otterburn in Redesdale, photographed by the Battlefields Trust as part of the Revitalising Redesdale project. The exact location of the battle remains uncertain, but this area north-west of Otterburn village is believed to be where most of the fighting took place. (Battlefields Trust)

Above left: The eighteenth-century Percy Cross at Otterburn, erected on or near the site of an earlier monument which has been dated to the fourteenth century. (Battlefields Trust)

Above right: This new interpretation board at Homildon Hill was erected in 2018. It shows the Scots deployed with their right flank on the level ground at the bottom of the slope, and their left on the saddle between Homildon and Harehope hills. The English main force is shown deployed in the vicinity of the Battle Stone with archers in the front rank, while a detached force of 'knights and men at arms' is facing the Scottish left.

Looking south from the English deployment area along the A697 towards the saddle between Homildon and Harehope hills. It is obvious that an enemy drawn up in the vicinity of the saddle would be well out of bow range from this position.

Looking in the opposite direction from the previous photo, from the Scottish position on the saddle at Homildon Hill down towards the English line. It was down this slope that Douglas and Swinton led their doomed charge.

The view from the slope of Harehope Hill across the saddle where the Scottish army was deployed. From this elevated position, the English archers were within range of the Scots and able to inflict severe damage on their close-packed formation. The shallow gully running into the woods in the middle distance was probably a minor obstacle to men on foot, but would have been sufficient to hamper the movements of heavily armoured cavalry.

The gatehouse or barbican of Alnwick Castle, which in its present form probably dates from the late fifteenth century. The threat from north of the border meant that even at this late date, fortifications in Northumbria were being energetically strengthened and extended.

The view upstream along the River Tweed from Coldstream village towards the location of the old ford near the confluence of the Tweed and the Leet Water. Edward I crossed by the ford on his invasion of Scotland in 1296, and James IV's army followed the same route in the opposite direction on its way to Flodden in 1513. The site of the Battle of Carham, fought nearly 500 years earlier, is less than 3 miles to the west.

Above left: The Battle of Flodden war memorial on Piper Hill, near the position where the English right wing was deployed, was erected in 1910. It is inscribed 'To the Dead of Both Nations'. (Megan Peers)

Above right: The battlefield of Flodden today, looking northwards from the ridge near the centre of the Scottish line. This is the view that James's artillerymen would have had, looking slightly downhill towards the opposite slope where the English army was deployed. The monument on Piper Hill can be seen in the middle distance, and beyond that the hills of Scotland. The Scots had been outmanoeuvred and forced to fight with their English opponents between them and their homeland, a factor which made their escape almost impossible once they were defeated on the field. (Megan Peers)

What Richard hoped to gain by calling up the entire English feudal levy, which would have included many men with no military training or equipment at all, has often been debated. Probably he intended simply to collect money in the form of scutage, a tax which had been an accepted alternative to personal military service since the twelfth century. In the event, Parliament objected strenuously and the whole idea was dropped, but the king nevertheless managed to muster a very large army for the invasion, numbering about 14,000, of whom most were archers. He crossed the border in August 1385, burnt the abbeys at Dryburgh, Melrose and Newbattle, and marched on to Edinburgh. His uncle, John of Gaunt, the Duke of Lancaster, went even further, burning Perth and Dundee, even threatening Aberdeen. But the Scots refused to be drawn into a pitched battle and withdrew their main forces into the Highlands, while a small force of French and Scots under Carrick and de Vienne raided into Cumbria. After two weeks of fruitless marching without bringing the enemy to battle, Richard decided to turn back towards London. The retirement was apparently against the advice of John of Gaunt, who wanted to move west across the Northumbrian hills to intercept Carrick's raiders, but according to Froissart, the Earl of Suffolk argued against this plan, claiming that John actually wanted Richard to fall into a Scottish ambush in the narrow defiles and be killed or captured, so that he could take the throne for himself.

However the Scottish raiding parties were repulsed by the garrison of Carlisle, and John instead negotiated another truce with the Scots, taking advantage of deteriorating relations between the Scottish soldiers and their French allies. Froissart says that the Scots were naturally unsociable, and also resented the presence of the foreigners because they feared that they would eat up all their supplies. This was perhaps inevitable in a relatively poor country where many people already lived hand to mouth, but the French made no secret of their view that the Scots were backward, and their country wild and primitive by continental standards. Furthermore, the locals were accused of charging excessive prices for essential supplies, while they in turn alleged that the French did not pay for what they consumed, but plundered the countryside and ruined their crops by carelessly riding through them. The visitors were also more enthusiastic about raiding into England, not having to live with the inevitable retaliation which this would bring upon the villages of Scotland, and tended to regard their allies' greater circumspection as cowardice. Things deteriorated so far that de Vienne was not allowed to leave Scotland until compensation had been paid for the damage that his men had caused, but in November 1385 the last French troops finally departed.

The Campaign of 1388

The truce held for nearly three years, but the Scots took the offensive once again in the summer of 1388. According to Froissart, they believed that the north of England would be vulnerable because King Richard II had recently removed Lord Nevill, who as Earl of Northumberland had been responsible for the security of the border, on suspicion of disloyalty, and replaced him with Henry Percy, the head of a family which had been prominent in the North since the time of William I. Carrick, James Earl of Douglas, and other Scottish lords held a conference at Aberdeen, without informing King Robert, at which they planned to assemble an army at Jedburgh ready to march at the beginning of August. Already, in June, Scottish seaborne raids had struck the Isle of Man and Carlingford in Ireland, both of which were held by the English. According to Walter Bower, the voyage was led by Sir William Douglas of Nithsdale and Sir Robert Stewart of Durisdeer (later captured at Homildon Hill), who seized the dilapidated castle at Carlingford and looted it, along with fifteen ships found in the harbour. They then returned to Galloway via the Isle of Man, arriving home 'well satisfied' with the huge amount of plunder they had taken. This has all the hallmarks of a well-planned diversionary operation, but we have no evidence that it was part of an overall master plan for the offensives against England, or even that such a plan existed. Froissart says that the Scots had intended simply to advance down the west coast and attack Carlisle, but that an English spy who was arrested in their camp revealed information which forced a change of plan.

The newly appointed Warden of the East March, responsible for the security of Berwick-upon-Tweed and the surrounding districts, was the 24-year-old son of Earl Henry of Northumberland, also named Henry Percy, distinguished from his father by the nickname 'Hotspur'. He had gathered a strong army at Newcastle, and if the Scots invaded in the west he intended to retaliate by attacking along the east coast and inflicting devastating damage on the undefended land of Lothian, which in Froissart's words was 'an open country, which can be entered anywhere' – a reference to the relative lack of castles on the Scottish side of the border. In order to prevent this, the Scots decided to split their forces and attack along both coasts simultaneously. As Armstrong (2006) points out, their assembly area, which was around Southdean Church, 6 miles south of Jedburgh and just across the border from the upper reaches of Redesdale, was ideally placed for an advance in either direction. Carrick was unable to take the field in person, as he had been disabled as a result of being kicked by a horse, so the main western column was led by the king's third son, Robert Stewart, Earl of Fife, and another member of the Douglas family, Sir Archibald Lord of Galloway, who was known as 'the Grim' on account of his 'terrible countenance'. In command of the eastern column was James, 2nd Earl of Douglas and Mar, a son-in-law of the king and head of the Douglas clan. Walter Bower, whose account is at variance with Froissart's in many respects, claims that rather than following an agreed plan, Douglas's independent attack in the east was an act of insubordination, contrary to his previous agreement to accompany Fife to Carlisle. However, Froissart's circumstantial account does seem to make more sense from a strategic point of view.

Douglas was accompanied by George Dunbar, the 3rd Earl of March, and his brother John Dunbar, 1st Earl of Moray, who between them commanded around 6,000 men, including perhaps 300 men-at-arms (Heath, 1982), drawn mainly from Lothian and the Borders. It is possible that they were all mounted, as indeed they must have been if Froissart's estimate that they travelled over 60 miles in twenty-four hours is accurate. In order to maintain the element of surprise, they were forbidden to attack or rob any settlement until they were south of the River Tyne. Peter Armstrong suggests that they entered English territory at the crossing point then called the Redeswire, a pass over the Cheviot Hills at the head of Redesdale, now known as Carter Bar. They must then have ridden down the dale as far as the village of Otterburn, then turned south-east across Ottercops Moss and then eastwards in the direction of Morpeth as far as Rothley Crags. From there, turning south, they crossed the River Tyne on 29 July upstream of Newcastle in the vicinity of Prudhoe. In support of this itinerary, Armstrong cites one of the old English ballads which are usually disregarded as historical sources, but the route is a plausible one which would have avoided the English garrisons and large centres of population, where the alarm would surely have been raised. As Froissart points out, it also took the raiders into territory owned by the Percy family, whose head, Henry, was now the most powerful man in the north of England. The Scottish manoeuvre would leave him with no option but to act to prevent the destruction of the family estates.

After crossing the Tyne, Douglas's men began to ravage the countryside around Durham, although the city itself was too well defended to be seriously threatened, the Bishop of Durham already assembling an army there to march to the relief of Newcastle. King Richard had apparently instructed the northern lords to await his arrival with the royal army, which in the event never appeared (Armstrong); this may be one reason why little resistance was offered to the Scots at this stage. Henry Percy senior remained inactive at Alnwick, while Henry Hotspur and his younger brother, Sir Ralph Percy, commanded the men assembled at Newcastle. This force seems to have outnumbered Douglas's column, as according to Froissart's account it included around 8,000 infantry and 600 men-at-arms. The chronicler gives the names of their commanders as Sir Ralph Lumley, Sir Mathew Redman of Westmoreland, the Captain of Berwick-upon-Tweed, Sir Robert Ogle, Sir Thomas Grey, Sir Thomas Holton, Sir John Felton, Sir John Lilleburn, Sir Thomas Abingdon, Sir John Coppledike, the seneschal of York, 'and divers other'.

After three days of plundering in County Durham, the Scots moved northward again and appeared outside the walls of Newcastle. By now they were slowed down by a huge herd of stolen cattle, which they intended to drive over the border, but Hotspur still declined to come out and meet them in battle. The reason for this uncharacteristic timidity, apart from the king's instructions, was probably that he was afraid of being lured into a trap. He could not have known the whereabouts of the main Scottish army under the Earl of Fife, and may have assumed that Douglas's weaker force was merely bait to lure him out so that Fife could overpower his men in open battle and seize Newcastle. In fact, Douglas's main aim was probably to gain time for the precious cattle to be driven on ahead into Scottish territory. Froissart, who enjoyed recounting tales of chivalry, tells how some of the knights skirmished outside the gates, and at one point Douglas and Hotspur engaged each other in single combat. This may seem an implausible story, though it does fit with the characters of both men as described by contemporaries. According to the chronicler, Douglas was victorious in the fight and captured Hotspur's lance pennon. The latter escaped with his life, but was 'sore displeased' by the humiliation of losing his lance's flag, assuring his opponent that he would not live to take the trophy out of Northumberland. Douglas replied that the pennon would be hanging outside his lodging that night if Hotspur cared to come and take it, but Froissart says that he was persuaded not to do so by his advisors, who – this time with justification – feared another trap.

The Battle of Otterburn

After two days the Scots suddenly withdrew, probably because they were aware of the approach of more English troops a day's march away to the south. These proved to be the relief force led by the Bishop of Durham. Douglas must also have known that the Earl of Fife's column had stalled outside Carlisle, and may have feared that this would allow Hotspur's father to move south from Alnwick and threaten his rear. So on 4 August, Douglas's men marched north by way of Ponteland Castle, which they seized along with its owner by a rapid assault and burned, then moved on up Redesdale to the vicinity of Otterburn, just over 30 miles from Newcastle. There they built a fortified camp and attempted to storm Otterburn Castle, but unlike those of Ponteland the defences resisted the initial assault. According to Froissart, Hotspur was warned by the local knights that Douglas's column was the main Scottish army, alleged to be 40,000 strong, and was at first reluctant to pursue. However he then received a report from scouts who had followed the enemy to Ponteland, who assured him that the Scots actually numbered no more than 3,000. Both figures were wildly inaccurate, but Hotspur must by now have realized that he had been bluffed by an inferior force. He therefore decided not to wait for the Bishop of Durham's reinforcements to arrive, but hurried in pursuit. The English army probably arrived at Otterburn during the evening of 5 August. There is some uncertainty about the date, because although most of the chroniclers agree on 5 August, Froissart dates it a fortnight later, on the 19th. Peter Armstrong points out that Froissart's date has the advantage that there would then have been a full moon, which would have made it easier to fight by night, but concludes that none of the sources mention the phase of the moon, and the *Westminster Chronicle* actually tells us that it was so dark that some of the English soldiers killed each other, mistaking their comrades for Scotsmen. (Froissart's account is inconsistent in this respect. He says that when the English first attacked the Scottish camp, the night was well advanced, but the moonlight made it almost as bright as day. In fact, it can hardly have been yet dark at this point. Later, when discussing Douglas's death, he tells us that there was 'no light but by the shining of the moon', but the implication is that this light was insufficient for Douglas's men to see and follow him.) Whatever the truth, given the need for the Scots to get back quickly over the border with their loot, and Hotspur's eagerness to catch them, it is difficult to see why either side would have hesitated for two weeks before moving off or giving battle.

Douglas had spent the previous day unsuccessfully laying siege to Otterburn Castle, despite the recommendation of most of his officers that he should abandon it and move to join the western column at Carlisle, having arguably accomplished his original mission. The reasons for his decision to ignore this advice are not entirely clear. In the late fourteenth century, a decisive battle was very much an exception to the usual pattern of border warfare. At this period, both sides seem to have adopted a policy of avoiding such encounters as far as possible, the Scots restricting themselves to what were essentially fast-moving raids and the English relying on fortifications to counter them (Grant, 1992). According to Froissart, however, Douglas thought it dishonourable to retire further without giving Hotspur the chance to meet him in battle and avenge the humiliation of the lost pennon, and the later ballads – which, as Grant has pointed out, may be historically inaccurate but are useful sources for contemporary frontier attitudes – are unanimous in treating the subsequent fight as the result of personal rivalry between the two men. It is of course also possible that Hotspur had simply taken Douglas by surprise with the speed of his pursuit, which may account for the apparently careless way in which the Scottish army was deployed. The servants, with the baggage and the stolen cattle, had a separate camp, which Froissart describes as being 'at the entrance of the marsh on the road to Newcastle'. This presumably means that it was on the lower ground near the River Rede, where the cattle could find grazing and water in the wet meadows. It is noteworthy that Froissart attributes the strength of Otterburn Castle to its situation in the marshes, which would have made it difficult to get heavy siege equipment within reach of the walls. These marshes have long since been drained, but the mention of the road suggests that the camp was in the vicinity of the modern A696, on the east bank of the Rede. The fighting troops had their own camp nearby, probably on the lower slopes of the hill called Blakeman's Law, where they were resting, having taken off most of their armour. Armstrong mentions one possible reason for this arrangement being the midges that no doubt haunted the wet places of Northumberland in the summer, just as they do today, and of course the cattle would also have attracted huge numbers of biting flies. So Douglas and his men-at-arms may well have thought that the greater comfort of a drier hilltop camp site outweighed the inconvenience of carrying water up from the river. We know that there was plenty of firewood available, because Froissart tells us that the men made huts for themselves from trees and branches as well as fortifying the camps with what was presumably a wooden palisade. Today there is a small copse at Percy's Cross and a larger wooded area on the other side of Otterburn village, but most of the area is open ground; in the 1380s, however, it seems to have had much more extensive tree cover.

The location was not in itself of any strategic value, and a shortage of supplies would have made it difficult for either army to sustain itself in the area for long – a point made eloquently by the *Ballad of Otterbourne* (Child, 1889). According to this admittedly late and largely unhistorical source, after defeating his opponent at Newcastle, Douglas had offered him a chance to redeem his fortunes, promising to wait for him at Otterburn for three days despite the difficulty of supplying his army there:

> 'The Otterbourne's a bonnie burn;
> 'Tis pleasant there to be;
> But there is nought at Otterbourne,
> To feed my men and me.

'The deer rins wild on hill and dale,
The birds fly wild from tree to tree;
But there is neither bread nor kale,
To feed my men and me.'

A near-contemporary monument, the Percy Cross, lies just outside Otterburn village at a location known as Battle Riggs, and is generally believed to mark the focal point of the battlefield, even though the exact location of the fighting remains uncertain (see the English Heritage battlefield report on Otterburn at historicengland.org.uk). Tyson (1992) points out that none of the authors of our primary sources were personally familiar with the area, and they are often in error about the topographical details. One of Froissart's informants, Jean de Cantiran, was present at the battle, in which he was captured, but the chronicler himself seems to have been very confused about the geography of Northumberland, as he states that Otterburn lay only 'eight short leagues' from Newcastle. A league was supposed to be the distance a man on foot could walk in an hour, which could hardly be more than 3 miles, but the actual distance between the two places is more than 30 miles. The only known grave pit thought to be associated with the battle was discovered in 1877 at St Cuthbert's Church, Elsdon, more than 2 miles from Percy's Cross, but as this was the parish church for the whole area at the time it would not be surprising if bodies, especially those of higher-status casualties, had been carried there to be interred. Fortunately from our point of view, of all the battles discussed in this book, Otterburn is the one in which the terrain had least influence on the outcome, so our understanding of events is not greatly affected by this uncertainty.

According to Bower's *Scotichronicon*, the Scots had sent out no scouts, which if true was an uncharacteristic omission, but would explain why the first intelligence they had of the English army was when a group of about a hundred men-at-arms and 700 infantry under Sir Mathew Redman charged into the servants' camp just as the sun was setting. It appears that Hotspur had marched directly up the valley along the road from Newcastle and was well aware that the Scots were camped somewhere in front of him, but had no idea that there were two camps. According to both John Hardyng and the *Westminster Chronicle*, Redman's mission had been to outflank the enemy and take them in the rear. He may have been under the misapprehension that he was already in the correct position, or might have attacked simply to clear an unexpected obstacle from his line of march, but he quickly became embroiled as the servants put up an unexpectedly strong resistance. As they were not intended to take their place in the line of battle, these men would not have worn any armour, but they were probably armed with a selection of the typical weapons of the Scottish common people – spears, knives, axes and perhaps the occasional bow or sword. There would also have been young squires among them, who had received some military training and had been sent to look after the horses. These men, together with the obstacles presented by the palisade and the marsh, were sufficient to hold Redman long enough for their comrades in the adjacent camp to realize what was happening.

Douglas's men were soon alerted by the noise of the fighting and the war cries of both sides. The English went into action shouting 'Percy! Percy!', to which the Scots replied 'Douglas!' Froissart says that the latter had already drawn up a plan of action in case of a surprise attack, and his troops reacted quickly, sending a contingent of soldiers without delay to reinforce the beleaguered servants, while their commander and the rest of his men hastily put on their armour. In fact, they never had time to complete the process, Wyntoun describing men who had to go into the fight lacking arm or leg protection, or in the case of the Earl of Moray, his helmet. The *Scotichronicon* says that they had all been dressed for a feast, being unarmed and wearing long gowns which were more comfortable in the summer heat than their normal campaigning attire. Meanwhile, Hotspur arrived in the vicinity of Percy's Cross with the English main body, and upon hearing the sound of fighting did not stop to deploy into formal battle array but dismounted his men and urged them on ahead in what the *Westminster Chronicle* describes as 'irregular order'. Bower quotes Thomas Barry as saying that the English archers were on one side, with their men-at-arms bunched together on the other. As they straggled along the road, Douglas suddenly appeared out of the trees on their right flank with the bulk of the Scottish army. Bower says that the leading men in Douglas's force were mounted, but they must have abandoned their horses before going into action, as all the combats described by Froissart seem to have been conducted on foot. In Wyntoun's words, 'the English men saw not his coming' until it was too late. Looking at the ground today, it seems that the approach of the Scots should have been clearly visible, but, as Armstrong points out, at the time the view of the lower slopes of Blakeman's Law was probably obscured by trees. It was in any case getting dark, and the attention of the English was fixed on the noise of battle to their front, where Redman was gradually breaking down the resistance in the servants' camp. It appears that Hotspur's archers had found themselves on the exposed right of the English army, because they had no time to deploy and shoot before the Scots were upon them, driving them back in confusion on the men-at-arms. After that, says Froissart, archery had no place in the fight on either side. This was of course a stroke of luck for Douglas's men, because they were able to get to close quarters and fight hand-to-hand, which as Froissart tells us was always their preferred tactic, without having to face the arrow storm which had stopped their predecessors at Dupplin Moor and Halidon Hill.

Nevertheless, the battle was far from over, because Hotspur now brought up the rest of his force to face Douglas and the bloody struggle continued into the night. For a while, the English forced the Scots back and came near to capturing Douglas's banner, which Froissart says would certainly have been lost but for the valour of two Sir Patrick Hepbourns – father and son – who fought beside the earl. The Westminster chronicler writes approvingly of the deeds of Sir Mathew Redman, who eventually forced the Scots facing him to flee and pursued them northwards towards the border, giving no quarter except to knights thought to be worth at least 100 marks in ransom money. His performance might be considered less creditable, however, in view of the fact that most of his opponents were poorly armed servants, and Froissart says that he in fact tried to make his escape alone and on horseback, as his companions had all been killed or captured by the reinforcements sent by Douglas. Whichever version we believe, his disappearance from the field left Hotspur in an even more difficult position.

Meanwhile, however, Douglas was receiving more effective support from his subordinates. The earls of March and Moray now brought up their contingents to join in the fight against Hotspur – 'from another part of the field', says Thomas Walsingham, though he does not tell us where they had been until then. Probably they had followed Douglas out of the camp as soon as they could. Douglas himself was in the thick of the action, swinging a great two-handed axe, but at some point during the fight he fell, mortally wounded. The *Ballad of Otterbourne* tells a lively tale of how Hotspur himself struck his opponent on the forehead with his sword, a blow that proved fatal because Douglas had forgotten his helmet in his haste to get into battle. Before he lost consciousness, the Scottish commander instructed his page to hide his body in a clump of bracken, so that his men might not learn of his death until after the battle. He had allegedly had a premonition of his own demise, recounted in what is probably the most famous verse in all of the medieval ballads:

> 'But I have dreamed a dreary dream,
> Beyond the Isle of Skye;
> I saw a dead man win a fight,
> And I think that man was I.'

In reality, no Englishman claimed credit for the deed, and according to Froissart none of the men who fought him realized that it was the Earl of Douglas whom they had slain. This chronicler describes his end in considerable detail, but his informants can only have reconstructed the events from the wounds later found on Douglas's body. He is said to have been struck by three spears – one in the shoulder, one in the thigh and another which glanced off his breastplate and wounded him in the stomach. Then, as he fell, someone hit him on the head with an axe and again on the thigh. Plate armour should have been better able to resist spear thrusts, but as we have seen it is likely that Douglas had left off some pieces of his armour in his haste. Froissart adds that the Scots remained unaware that their leader had fallen, which was fortunate because they might have become demoralized and fled if the news had spread. But some of Douglas's followers certainly knew that he was hurt, because the same source tells how the knights James Lindsay and John and Walter Sinclair – with the earl's chaplain, William of North Berwick – found him lying wounded and picked up his banner, whose bearer was also grievously hurt. The chaplain, who had followed his master throughout the battle and joined in the fighting with an axe in his hands, was later rewarded for his courage by being made Archdeacon of Aberdeen. Meanwhile, Sir Ralph Percy had fought his way far ahead of the English lines, but was eventually overpowered and captured, badly wounded and losing blood. His captor, Sir John Maxwell, handed him over to the Earl of Moray, who ordered his men to stop the bleeding and bandage his wounds. However, another Englishman, a squire named Thomas Waltham, who had taken an oath that he would do the greatest deeds in his next battle or die in the attempt, refused all demands to surrender when he was surrounded, and was eventually killed.

Finally, the English began to give way, the Scots pushing forward and breaking through their line. Walter Bower identifies a Scottish knight, Sir John Swinton, as playing a decisive role in the melee. An exceptionally powerful man, he moved out to one flank as the battle lines clashed, and from there he advanced along the front of the Englishmen, striking their levelled lances to the ground with his own spear so that his compatriots could get in the first blow. It was this unconventional manoeuvre, according to Bower, that forced Hotspur's men to fall back for the last time, although Froissart ascribes their defeat mainly to the fact that they were more tired than the Scots after their breakneck journey from Newcastle. Hotspur was seen fighting a protracted duel with the Scottish knight Sir John Montgomery of Eaglesham, but none of his men was able to go to his assistance and he was forced to surrender. Those of his men who did not follow his example then broke and fled south, pursued by the Scots for about 5 leagues. Froissart says that if the victors had been more numerous, none of the English would have escaped, but a few miles further on the fugitives met the Bishop of Durham marching to their aid with another 7,000 men. The bishop, says Froissart, did his best to help the beaten men, but the news that they brought of an overwhelming Scottish victory spread panic in his army. Many of the English soldiers turned and fled back towards Newcastle and the crossings of the River Tyne, and the knights who remained advised their commander that he had no option but to retreat. Froissart says that it was the opinion of many that the bishop could still have turned the tide of the battle if he had managed to rally the fugitives and counterattack, but in truth it was all he could do to protect Newcastle. The next day he rallied his men and led them north again, but found the enemy still in their strong defensive position at Otterburn. At the same time, the surviving Scottish leaders, whose scouts had informed them of the approach of the English force, assembled their men and ordered them all to blow on the horns which they carried around their necks, making a noise which no doubt made them seem more numerous than they were, spreading fear among the already demoralized English troops. Once again, the bishop decided not to risk an attack, but led his men back to Newcastle.

According to Froissart, when Sir Mathew Redman escaped from the field, he was pursued by a Scottish knight, Sir James Lindsay, who eventually overtook him and after a long hand-to-hand fight took him prisoner. Lindsay sent him back to Newcastle on parole, in return for which Redman promised to present himself at Edinburgh within three weeks. However, Lindsay lost his way on his return and blundered into the Bishop of Durham's army, whereupon he was himself captured.

The two men later met at Newcastle and agreed in effect to exchange each other, so that both regained their freedom without any ransom being paid. Redman, says the chronicler (Froissart), was one of 1,040 prisoners taken by the Scots, in addition to 1,840 dead and more than a thousand badly wounded. For their part, the Scots lost 100 dead and 200 captured, most of the latter being taken during the pursuit, when a few of the English turned on those who had advanced too far ahead of their comrades. Bower gives a similar figure of 1,500 Englishmen killed, but the *Westminster Chronicle* suggests that the losses were far more equal and that each side lost somewhere between 500 and 550 men. None of these figures are necessarily reliable. Armstrong argues that no English knights, and only one squire, are mentioned by name as having been killed, which means that almost all of those present must have surrendered. Of course, their opponents would have been happy to take men of rank as prisoners because of the prospect of ransom, and Froissart confirms that they were treated with courtesy. The fate of common soldiers, whose families could not afford to ransom them, is likely to have been very different, and they must have comprised the bulk of the casualties, whatever figure we accept.

Later English sources tended to play down the scale of the defeat. Thomas Walsingham suggests that the Scots had suffered so badly in the battle that they returned home as soon as they could, and subsequently did not dare to return to England. John Hardyng even gives the impression that – apart from the unfortunate capture of Henry Percy – the English had the best of it. More recent English historians have often regarded the battle as having little long-term significance. For example, Colonel A.H. Burne considered that 'never was battle fought on English soil that had less effect on the fortunes of Old England' (Burne, 1952). Certainly, it seems to have had little effect on the course of the rest of the 1388 campaign. The Scottish western column led by the Earl of Fife had ravaged the Eden Valley and collected its own haul of cattle and prisoners for ransom, but Fife had failed to capture Carlisle and withdrew soon after the battle at Otterburn. Richard II made plans to march north again, but was unable to raise the money for a fresh army, and in June 1389 he was obliged to sign a peace treaty with both France and Scotland. The latter was spared another invasion, but gained nothing apart from the ransom money that was received for the prisoners, and even that went mostly to individual knights and not to the crown. Henry Hotspur, for example, paid 7,000 marks for his freedom, and Sir John Montgomery used the money to build Polnoon Castle in Renfrewshire. His former prisoner is said to have become a firm friend, and even advised Sir John on the defences of his new seat. The body of James Douglas was taken back to Melrose Abbey and buried there. He was succeeded as earl by Archibald 'the Grim'.

From a Scottish point of view, however, the victory provided a much-needed boost to national morale after a long series of defeats at the hands of the English. Grant (1992) even sees Otterburn as one of the most important battles of the Hundred Years' War, in that it accentuated the war-weariness that was already growing in England and gave rise to a sense that final victory in a war on two fronts might be permanently out of reach. Consequently, it could be said to have led directly to the peace negotiations which culminated in the twenty-eight-year truce agreed with Charles VI of France in 1396. Only six years after that, however, the verdict of the battle was to be dramatically reversed in an encounter which saw many of the same participants facing each once again.

Otterburn stands out among the sites discussed in this book because of its remoteness from large centres of population. Carham was fought in the wide, fertile valley of the River Tweed, Halidon Hill and the encounters at Alnwick on the outskirts of the towns of the coastal plain, Homildon Hill and Flodden on the boundaries between the plain and the hills. But Upper Redesdale, where the Battle of Otterburn was fought, is a very different landscape, wilder and more rugged. The journey up Redesdale towards the Scottish border is in fact worth making today for its scenic interest alone. The village of Otterburn is situated on the A696, which runs north-east from Newcastle to join the A68 to Jedburgh just north of the battle site. It is not easily reachable by public transport, although occasional buses do run from both Newcastle and Jedburgh. The area is covered by the 1:25,000-scale Ordnance Survey Explorer map number OL42, as well as the 1:50,000 Landranger map number 80. The Percy Cross (grid reference NY877936) marks the traditional site of the battle near the village, though it should be remembered that doubts remain about the exact location of the encounter. The sandstone cross itself is a Grade II listed building, which according to the Historic England listing entry was erected in 1777 to replace an earlier structure which had long since fallen down. The base has been dated to the fourteenth century (historicengland.org.uk) and is presumed to have belonged to the original monument. However, James Robson (1897) quotes Robert White, whose *History of the Battle of Otterburn* was published in 1857 and who cites a map of 1769 as evidence that the original cross had been 'about 180 paces east from the present cross'. The landowner, says White, had erected the new monument where it could be seen from the turnpike road, which opened in the same year as the cross was built. According to the same source, the medieval base was in fact an old architrave which was taken from the kitchen at Otterburn Hall. The site of Otterburn Castle is now occupied by the Otterburn Tower Hotel in the village itself. There is a public right of way across the battlefield, which is marked on the OS maps, and the 3½-mile walk suggested by Rupert Matthews (2008) follows this route, but the Battlefields Trust website recommends the pedestrian route via Otterburn Hall Farm, which is at grid reference NY882943.

Chapter Six

'The Most Worthy Knight': Homildon Hill, 1402

Date	14 September 1402
Location	Homildon Hill, near Wooler, Northumberland
Combatants	English under Henry Percy, Earl of Northumberland, versus Scots led by Sir Archibald, 4th Earl of Douglas
Outcome	English victory

SEVERAL OF THE protagonists in the Otterburn campaign were still on the scene when the next major confrontation took place in 1402. King Robert II of Scotland had died in 1390 and was succeeded by his son, John of Carrick, who took the title of King Robert III. (The name John had unfortunate associations for Scottish royalty ever since the reign of the puppet king, John Balliol.) Robert II had not been a very effective ruler; he had allowed magnates such as the notorious Wolf of Badenoch to run riot in the remoter areas of the kingdom, leading to the damning verdict of one chronicle, written at Elgin Cathedral, that 'there was no law in Scotland' during his reign. Robert III was no better. He was in his mid-50s when he came to the throne and in poor health, so parliament did not consider him fit to govern; his brother, Robert Stewart, Earl of Fife – who had led the western column in the Otterburn campaign – was appointed as Lieutenant, or regent. In 1393, a council returned power to the king in association with his son, David, Duke of Rothesay, who was formally made Lieutenant in 1399, while Fife was compensated with the title of Duke of Albany. In 1401, Albany staged a coup with the aid of his supporters in parliament, among whom was Sir Archibald Douglas, the son of Albany's old comrade in arms, Archibald 'the Grim', and a strong advocate of an anti-English foreign policy. They imprisoned Rothesay, and Albany regained the title of Lieutenant. In March of the following year, Rothesay died in suspicious circumstances, but a general council exonerated Albany, who became the effective ruler of Scotland until his death eighteen years later.

One of the noblemen alienated by this blatant power struggle was George Dunbar, the Earl of March, who had been one of the principal architects of the victory at Otterburn. Dunbar's daughter had been married to Rothesay, but owing to an irregularity in the ceremony, the Pope had been obliged to issue a dispensation allowing them to remarry after a token separation. Albany, however, declared the marriage contract annulled and, whether of his own free will or not, Rothesay ended up marrying Marjory, the daughter of the Earl of Douglas. George Dunbar responded to this humiliation by taking his entire family into exile in England, where – there having also been a change of leadership south of the border – he offered his allegiance to the new king, Henry IV. In 1399, Richard II had tried to prevent Henry Bolingbroke, the son of the late John of Gaunt, from inheriting his father's lands and title. Henry, who was already in exile in France, responded by raising an army and landing in Yorkshire while Richard was campaigning in Ireland. Among those who sympathized with him was Henry Hotspur's father, Henry Percy, the Earl of Northumberland, who – despite being responsible as Warden for the security of the north of England – allowed Bolingbroke to march southwards unimpeded. Bolingbroke seems initially only to have aimed to reclaim his inheritance, but Richard's supporters melted away, and upon his return from Ireland the king had no choice but to surrender. Bolingbroke imprisoned his predecessor in the Tower of London, and on 13 October 1399 he was crowned as King Henry IV of England. Richard had been promised his life in exchange for his throne, but was subsequently murdered, apparently by starvation in Pontefract Castle in Yorkshire.

Henry Hotspur's career had not suffered on account of his mishap at Otterburn, and in 1394 he had been sent across the Channel by

Richard II to govern the province of Aquitaine. In the following year, he accompanied the king on his expedition to Ireland. Despite the favour shown to him by Richard, however, he followed his father in transferring his allegiance to Henry IV, and in 1401 he was sent to command the forces fighting the rebellion of Owain Glyndwr in North Wales. Henry Bolingbroke's blatant usurpation was by no means universally popular, and he spent much of his reign suppressing a series of such rebellions. Rumours spread that Richard was not dead, but had escaped and was living at the Scottish court, and as early as January 1400 some of his supporters hatched a plot to assassinate Henry. Glyndwr's uprising was originally a local affair, provoked mainly by a land dispute between him and an English neighbour, but by September 1400 much of North Wales was in revolt and Owain was proclaiming himself Prince of Wales. When Hotspur arrived, he realized that the rebels were too strong to be easily overcome and he negotiated a truce on his own authority, but the king overruled him. Another hastily arranged ceasefire was no more successful, and by the beginning of 1402 the Welsh had inflicted several defeats on English forces and the war was beginning to spread out of control.

Meanwhile, as one of the new Scottish regent's leading henchmen, Archibald Douglas was given free rein to pursue his anti-English policy, and the Welsh revolt seemed to provide him with an excellent opportunity. The Scottish chronicler Walter Bower hints at the existence of an ambitious plan for an alliance between the Welsh and the Scots which aimed to expel the English from Britain altogether (Breverton, 2013): 'The Britons shall flourish, in alliance with the Alban people; the whole island will bear its ancient name.' This prospect might have been a useful rallying cry for many in both these ostensibly Celtic nations, but it is unlikely that the leaders of either thought it a realistic aim. The Scottish contribution turned out to be not much more than the usual cross-border raid. In June 1402, Sir Archibald Douglas sent raiding parties into Cumberland and Northumberland, but one of these was intercepted and defeated on its return journey at Nisbet, near Duns in Berwickshire. The victors in this skirmish were English troops from Berwick commanded by George Dunbar, the renegade Earl of March, and among the Scottish casualties was the younger Sir Patrick Hepbourn, another of the heroes of Otterburn. Then in August, Douglas marched south at the head of an army which Walter Bower estimated at 10,000 men, heading for Newcastle. His second in command was Albany's son, Murdoch Stewart, who was known by the title of Master of Fife. After gathering the usual haul of stolen cattle and other plunder, the Scots turned for home, marching along the edge of the hills and heading for the crossing of the Tweed at Coldstream. After passing through the small town of Wooler, they found their way blocked by an English army deployed at Milfield, 5 miles further on. Its commanders were Earl Henry of Northumberland, his son, Henry Hotspur, and George Dunbar. The only source other than Bower to give the numbers of the respective armies is the *Historia Vitae et Regni Ricardi Secundo* (Stow, ed., 1977), which states that the Scots had 12,000 or 13,000 men, while the English numbered 12,000 men-at-arms and 7,000 archers. Considering that this force was raised almost entirely from the border counties, the number of English men-at-arms seems excessively large, but it is at least likely that their army was numerically the stronger. Consequently, Douglas decided not to attack it head on, but to retire to a strong defensive position and let his enemy make the first move.

There are two detailed sources for the battle that followed: Walter Bower's *Scotichronicon* and Thomas Walsingham's *Historia Anglicana*. On the whole they are in agreement as far as the course of events is concerned, but unfortunately they are unclear about some of the topographical details, which means that different interpretations of the armies' deployment, and hence about the tactics used, are still possible. Thus three very different interpretations of the battle are still current. In the version favoured by Armstrong (2006), the Scots withdrew to the summit of Homildon Hill and took refuge in the ruins of an ancient hill fort, where the English archers virtually surrounded them and then shot them down from a distance. Bower says that

Douglas's men 'climbed to some rising ground called Homildon', while Walsingham states that they selected 'a hill near the town of Wooler, called Halweden Hil'. However, neither source specifically says that they climbed to the very top of the hill. This would have placed the action a very long way from the bottom of the slope, where the English were deployed. Bower says that the latter drew up 'on the plain facing the Scots', which presumably means that they could see the enemy positions, while Walsingham reports that upon seeing the Scottish deployment they 'left the road'. Assuming that the road followed roughly the same route as the A697 does now, along the edge of the level ground and around the bottom of the range of hills, this would put the English in a position from which any activity on the summit itself is not clearly visible. The proposed Scottish position is also most impractical from a defensive point of view. Traces of the hill fort can still be seen; it consists of a Bronze Age enclosure within an earth bank, with a smaller but better-preserved Iron Age construction within it, surrounded by a stone wall. Neither is in good enough condition today to be a viable defensive obstacle, nor are they likely to have been in 1402. The banks might have been useful as temporary corrals for livestock, but any advantage would seem hardly to have been worth the trouble of driving them all the way to the summit while under pressure from a pursuing force. In any case, there would have been no escape route from the position, and it is hard to see why an experienced general like Douglas would have detoured so far uphill just to place himself in a trap.

Consequently, both the alternative interpretations of the battle place the Scots about halfway up the slope of Homildon Hill, or more precisely on and around the saddle of lower ground between Homildon and Harehope Hill, its neighbour to the west, approximately at grid reference NT9637028762. Here, there is an area of relatively level ground where an army could have been deployed, and from where there is a clear line of sight to the road below. But the distance from the English line to the Scots' positions would still have been at least 400 yards, far greater than effective bow range. Bower goes on to say that Hotspur – having apparently forgotten the lesson of Otterburn – wanted to advance up the hill and attack immediately. However, Dunbar argued that they should instead 'send archers' to soften them up first. This source does not say exactly where they were to be sent, but the implication is clear that they had to change their position because they were not originally within range of the Scots. Walsingham gives some more details, but they confuse rather than clarify the issue. In Myers's translation (1969), when they saw the Scottish deployment, 'our men … left the road in which they had been opposing the Scots and climbed a hill facing the Scots'. Then the archers, 'drawn up in the dale', shot volleys of arrows at the Scottish schiltrons in order to provoke them to attack. The outnumbered Scottish archers returned the fire, but were quickly outshot and forced to flee.

The *Scotichronicon*'s version is rather different. Bower does not mention the Scottish archers, but says that the English bowmen, 'advancing towards the Scots', shot arrows that pinned their opponents' hands to their own lances, implying that their targets were either men-at-arms or the common soldiers in the schiltrons, since archers would not have carried spears. So we have two alternative accounts of the same English manoeuvre, which is unfortunate as it seems to have been this move that turned the tide of the battle. Walsingham apparently has the English volley shot either from their main position on the flat ground at the bottom of the Homildon Hill or from an advanced position on the lower slopes, which must mean either that the archer force was split or that any men who were sent further were not archers but men-at-arms. On the other hand, Bower implies that a force of archers was sent forward to engage the enemy main body, but does not say by what route. A tour of the battlefield shows that the only logical route by which this detachment could have gained a position on another 'hill facing the Scots' was on the English right flank, by climbing the neighbouring summit of Harehope Hill to emerge in a position on the left flank of Douglas's line, and the modern adherents of both alternative versions of events tend to agree on this at least.

Robert Hardy (Strickland & Hardy, 2005, pp.314–15) argued eloquently that the archers must have engaged the Scots from the front, advancing up Homildon Hill in order to do so, rather than from Harehope on the flank. In support of this, he cited a revised interpretation of Thomas of Walsingham by Professor John Childs of the English Heritage Battlefields Panel (see also Hardy, 2017). Their argument hinges on the exact meaning of Walsingham's remarks, because the original Latin is somewhat ambiguous. The text says '*montem Scotis oppositum concenderent*', which could mean that 'they climbed a hill opposite the Scots' but might also be interpreted as 'they climbed the hill facing the Scots'. 'The hill' might then refer to Homildon Hill itself. However, it must be concluded that there is simply not enough information in any of the written sources to enable us to rule out either hypothesis. Indeed, a new interpretation board unveiled by the Duke of Northumberland in 2018 gives an account of the battle which differs somewhat from either, showing the Scots deployed at an angle to the slope of the hill, with their right on the level ground at the bottom and their refused left on the saddle between Homildon and Harehope hills. The English main force is drawn up on the level ground along the road with the archers in the front rank, while a force of 'knights and men at arms' is shown facing the Scottish left flank, some distance down the slope from the saddle between the two hills. This interpretation has been endorsed by the Battlefields Trust project led by Clive Hallam-Baker and Geoffrey Carter (Carter, pers. comm.), but some uncertainties still remain.

However, it is perhaps possible to shed further light on the issue by a careful examination of the ground. The intervening slope between the two main opposing forces is fairly steep and generally convex, and it ends abruptly in a sudden drop at the bottom of Homildon Hill before meeting the flat ground, leaving little room for uncertainty about the position of the English battle line. But 400 yards is much too far for effective archery, especially when shooting uphill, and if the English had advanced much closer in a direct line up the hill they would have had an even worse view of the enemy position, thanks to the convexity of the slope. Yet in Bower's account their shooting was very effective, penetrating armour and causing numerous casualties. On the other hand, if the English were shooting from somewhere on the flank of Harehope Hill they would have enfiladed the enemy at around half that range, and at 200 yards their arrows might reasonably have achieved the sort of results that Bower describes. This is still a considerable range for a pre-gunpowder weapon, but the bow was particularly suited to such a situation. The impact of any missile depends principally on the velocity of the projectile, but also partly on its mass, which explains why in the era of the musket, men were often struck at long range by balls which lodged in their clothing or otherwise did little harm. A musket ball is relatively small and light, so once air resistance has slowed it down it retains little capacity for damage. (D.P. Miller, D. Allsop and D.J. Carr, 'The ballistics of seventeenth-century musket balls', *Journal of Conflict Archaeology*, 14:1, 2019, report the average weight of musket balls recovered from the battlefield of Edgehill in 1642 as 37.9 grams.) But an arrow is heavier (Mark Stretton, 2018, used reproduction arrows varying between 75 and 102 grams), and if it reaches its target at all the sharpened head is still able to inflict a wound. Because of its weight and low initial speed, it has to be shot on a curved trajectory in order to reach a target 200 yards away, so the men on Harehope Hill would have aimed slightly higher than their targets, allowing the arrows to drop on them from above. The weight of the missiles would have allowed them to pick up speed as they fell, so that they struck with almost as much energy as they would have had at point-blank range. This would have been how the archers managed to pin the hands of the Scottish spearmen to their weapons, as described by Bower. Elizabeth I's High Marshal, Sir Thomas Wilford, who was arguing for the continued usefulness of the bow as late as 1590, put it like this: 'only with the weight and fall [the arrow] galleth both horse and man, and though the wound be not mortal, yet both horse and man are made unserviceable' (quoted in Strickland & Hardy, 2005, Chapter 20). It is also difficult to envisage troops other than archers being very effective in such a flanking position. A small stream runs across the saddle between the two hills, and even today much of the lower ground is boggy. Rupert Matthews (2008) calls the feature a 'ravine', which rather overstates its significance, but it would have been a significant enough obstacle to impede any cavalry charge against the flanks of the Scottish schiltrons, and heavily armoured men-at-arms on foot would surely have been slowed down enough to reduce the effect of their attack.

Walsingham tells us that once the Scottish archers had been driven off, the Earl of Douglas took up his lance and rode 'down the hill' towards the English line. This implies that he attacked straight ahead, towards the road at the foot of Homildon Hill, and not to his left across the saddle towards the enemy on Harehope. Hardy interpreted this as evidence that the archers who were inflicting casualties on his men were therefore stationed to his front, but this would not necessarily have been the case. It would have been even more difficult for him to have attacked on horseback across the saddle towards Harehope Hill, first through a marsh and then up a steep slope, than it would have been for the English to advance in the opposite direction. On the other hand, a swift move straight downhill would have quickly taken him out of range of the flanking archers and given him the opportunity of engaging Hotspur's main body, which was surely his only chance of winning the battle. Unfortunately for him, the archers on Harehope were evidently only a detachment, and many more of the English bowmen were stationed at the bottom of Homildon with Percy. According to Thomas of Walsingham, these men fell back before the Scottish charge, but continued to shoot so effectively that they 'pierced the armour, perforated the helmets, pitted the swords, split the lances, and pierced all the equipment with ease'. Douglas received five wounds and was captured, and the casualties among his followers were so severe that not one of them reached the enemy line and no English knight was even wounded. This was despite the fact that, as Walsingham tells us, the Scottish knights had been 'improving their armour for three years'. This may have been done with the help of equipment supplied by their French allies, whose armour, according to Froissart's account of the Otterburn campaign (see Chapter Five, p.76), was superior to that usually worn by the Scots. Walter Bower, however, again gives a rather different account. According to his version, it was Sir John Swinton, the hero of Otterburn, who inspired the Scots to charge. In a passionate speech, he accused his countrymen of having been bewitched, being prepared to stand there helplessly while they were shot down like penned deer. Another Scotsman, Adam de Gordon of that Ilk (meaning of the Gordon estate, the term being used to avoid repetition), had pursued a deadly feud with Swinton for many years, but he was so impressed with his enemy's eloquence that he proclaimed him 'the most worthy knight in arms in the whole of Britain' and knelt to ask for his pardon, 'so that he might be girded as a knight by the hands of the same Sir John'. The two men then led the charge down the hill, followed by a hundred other men-at-arms, who inflicted 'a great slaughter' on the English before the attackers were all killed.

Understandably, this episode has often been cited as yet more evidence for the decisive superiority of the English longbow, but it does raise a number of questions. Firstly, it is difficult to see how the archers could have kept up their deadly shooting while retreating, as Walsingham says, because they could hardly have shot backwards while running, nor have stood and waited until an attacking horseman was at close range without running the risk of being ridden down if they failed to stop him. More usually in battles of the period – see, for example, Halidon Hill above and Froissart's account of Crecy – they seem to have stood their ground and shot without moving, and even then they seldom succeeded in stopping an enemy charge before it reached the men-at-arms. Unless Bower's account of the slaughtered English is entirely fictional, some at least of the archers must have been ridden down as they fell back, which means that Douglas and his men did get as far as Percy's battle line, or at least close enough to drive in a body of archers deployed across the front of it. It is noteworthy that the tactic which was so successful at Halidon Hill, of alternating units of archers and men-at-arms along the line so that they could support each other, is not mentioned here. Of course, if there were only a hundred Scottish knights involved, they would have been greatly outnumbered and the archers would have been able to concentrate their shooting from three sides as they drove into the English position on a narrow frontage. This might also explain the effectiveness of the archery against armour, because arrows could not normally be relied upon to penetrate plate armour, and certainly not helmets, at anything but the shortest of ranges (Strickland & Hardy, 2005; Stretton, 2018).

When they saw the fate of their knights, the rest of the Scots who remained on the hill – presumably mostly the outclassed archers and the poorly armoured spearmen – tried to escape. Bower relates that 'some Englishmen' had said that if the rest of the Scots had followed their superiors down the hill with the same enthusiasm they would have won the day, but they had suffered too badly at the hands of the English archers, by which are presumably meant those stationed on their flank on Harehope Hill. The latter were now positioned between the fleeing Scots and their homes, which may be why, as Walsingham says, it was the archers who led the pursuit and took many of them prisoner. Other Scots escaped them and got as far as the River Tweed, where 500 of them were said to have been drowned in their panic-stricken haste to cross. Nevertheless, many prisoners of rank were taken, for whom Hotspur and his nobles could expect lucrative ransoms. They were therefore indignant when King Henry, who was always desperate for new ways of raising money, decreed that all the prisoners should be handed over to him. This was the last straw for the Percys, who were already unhappy about being implicated in the murder of Richard II, and furthermore had been deprived of the lands which the new king had promised them in return for their support. Consequently, early in 1403, they renounced their allegiance to Henry and came out in revolt. Hotspur marched south to rendezvous with his uncle, Thomas Percy, who was Earl of Worcester, and the rebels met the king in battle at Shrewsbury on 21 July. Both sides employed large numbers of archers, and the storm of arrows claimed several eminent victims on both sides, as well as around 5,000 common soldiers. Henry's son, Henry, Prince of Wales – the future Henry V – was seriously wounded in the face, and Hotspur received a similar wound when he unwisely raised his visor during a desperate attempt to kill the king. Percy's wound was fatal, and when the news of his death spread the rebel army disintegrated. Thomas Percy was captured and beheaded. The king had Hotspur's body disinterred and cut into quarters, one of which was put on display at Newcastle, while his head ended up on a spike at York. His father, the earl, managed to escape a charge of treason as he had not personally participated in the rebellion, but five years later he did lead an army against the king and was killed at the Battle of Bramham Moor in Yorkshire. The Percy lands and titles were forfeited to the crown and their role in the North was taken over by the Neville family, whose head, Ralph, was made Earl of Westmorland. It was not until the Wars of the Roses in the late fifteenth century and the consequent fall of the Nevilles that the Percys fully regained their position (Rose, 2002). Henry Hotspur is commemorated by a modern statue on Pottergate in Alnwick, which was erected to mark the 700th anniversary of the family's occupation of Alnwick Castle.

The site of Homildon Hill (now better known as Humbleton Hill) is about 2 miles from the town of Wooler. It is not well marked on the ground, and the best overall view is obtained from the adjacent hills. Wooler is the nearest town to the battlefield, and can be reached by bus from Berwick or Morpeth. The A697 from Wooler to Coldstream runs along the bottom of the hills, roughly following the line along which the English main army was originally drawn up. The Bendor Stone or Battle Stone, which is to be found in a field just north of the road at grid reference NT968294, is often associated with the battle of 1402, and in the words of the Historic England battlefield report now 'serves as a monument' to it (historicengland.org.uk). However, it was not erected for this purpose, and in fact it probably dates from the Bronze Age, more than 2,000 years earlier. It would of course have been a prominent landmark at the time of the battle, just as it is now, so it may have served as a rallying point. The occasional bus between Wooler and Milfield may drop you on request at the turn-off to the village of Humbleton. Alternatively, a 2-mile walk from Wooler will take you through Humbleton and onto a track which leads west across the open slopes of Homildon Hill. The new interpretation board can be found near the point where the track leaves the road. Follow the track westwards for about a mile and you will arrive on the saddle between the two hills (grid reference NT963287), which most versions of the battle place at the centre of the fighting.

Chapter Seven

The Border Castles

THE CASTLE, IN the sense of a self-contained fortified building as distinct from the walls or towers designed to protect a town or city, was essentially a Norman introduction into England. Although the earlier Anglo-Saxon kings had developed a strategy based on fortified towns or burghs, which they used to great effect against the Viking invaders, they had no castles as the term was understood on the continent. Indeed, the chronicler Orderic Vitalis regarded the English lack of castles as an important factor in their defeat by the Normans. The first such structures in Western Europe appeared in northern France in the tenth century, and by the time William the Conqueror arrived in England in 1066, they had become a vital feature of French and Norman warfare (Bradbury, 1992). The newcomers lost no time in erecting new ones as soon as they arrived in a conquered district. At first these were temporary structures of what is known as the motte and bailey design, consisting of a wooden keep on top of a high mound, which could be a natural feature if one was available, but more often was an artificial hill made of earth. Before the end of the eleventh century, many of these, especially in the more vulnerable locations, were being rebuilt in stone (Gravett, 2003). Castles were designed not only to protect their owners and their households, but to provide a secure refuge from which mounted soldiers could operate to control the surrounding district, deploying a formidable combination of mobility and defensive strength.

By the beginning of the fifteenth century, Northumberland had the highest density of castles of any county in England. A survey commissioned in 1415 by Henry V, who was anxious to secure his northern border before embarking on his invasion of France, recorded thirty-seven castles, seventy-five towers and three 'fortalices' – a term which denoted a small fortress or fortified dwelling (King, 2007). However, as Dr King points out, most of these edifices were not recorded a century earlier, implying that the fourteenth century had seen an unprecedented increase in the number of defensive structures. The obvious explanation is the threat of Scottish raids, which had been an intermittent problem at least since the outbreak of Edward I's war in 1296, though Dr King questions this. Instead, he suggests that, just as in less turbulent parts of the country, the main function of the smaller castles at least was more that of displaying their owners' wealth and enhancing their social prestige. As evidence, he points to an apparent boom in castle building even at times when the border seemed to be at peace and the Scottish threat at least temporarily removed, such as after the defeat of William Wallace in 1298 or the capture of King David II at Neville's Cross in 1346. He also cites the unsuitability of many of the buildings, with their thin walls and wide window openings, for withstanding a serious siege. This trend would of course simply bring Northumberland into line with developments elsewhere in England, where, for example, the houses of the thirteenth- and fourteenth-century gentry were often embellished with moats which were discontinuous, overlooked by high banks, or for various other reasons were of no defensive value (Rackham, 1986, Chapter 16).

Nevertheless, many of the larger castles were built for a serious military role, and several of them withstood frequent attacks from across the border. Here we will look in more detail at the stories of just a representative few. Alnwick, already the nemesis of two Scottish kings, eventually became one of the most important strongholds in Northumberland. The de Vescy family held it for more than a century after the last of the two battles discussed in Chapter Two. One of its owners, Eustace de Vescy, had a particularly eventful career. A political opponent of King John, who reigned from 1199–1216, Eustace defected to the Scots in 1212 after being accused of treason, but Pope Innocent III ordered John to reinstate him. In 1213, he was allowed to return to Alnwick, but the king issued secret orders for the castle to be destroyed before he could do so. Evidently this was not done, but Eustace rebelled again in the First Barons' War of 1215, and was one of the magnates who forced John to sign the charter of rights known as Magna Carta. In the following year, he transferred his allegiance to the French dauphin, Louis the Lion – the future Louis VIII – who had staked a claim to the English throne, and accompanied a Scottish army which was marching south to support Louis against John. When they passed Barnard Castle in County Durham, which was held by a supporter of John, Hugh de Balliol, they decided to attack it, but Eustace carelessly rode within range of the walls while reconnoitring and was killed by an arrow through the head. Eustace forfeited his estates, but his son, William, regained royal favour during the reign of John's son, Henry III, and the family remained in possession of Alnwick until 1296, when their line died out and the castle went to the Bishop of Durham.

In 1309, the bishop sold it to Henry, 1st Baron Percy, whose descendants have held it ever since. Percy was a descendant of a Norman aristocrat and had served with distinction in Edward I's wars in Scotland. In 1328, his son, the 2nd Baron Percy, also named Henry, was appointed to the position of Lord Warden of the Marches, which in effect made Alnwick Castle the military headquarters of the whole border region. This Henry went on to fight at both Halidon Hill and Neville's Cross, and King Richard II rewarded the family's loyal service in 1377 by creating his grandson, Henry, 4th Baron Percy, the 1st Earl of Northumberland. The relations between the Percys and the man who overthrew Richard, Henry IV, have been discussed in Chapter Six. The castle had been provided with its present curtain walls and towers by the 1360s at the latest. During the Wars of the Roses of the late fifteenth century, it changed hands several times, but it was never taken by assault. Both the 2nd and 3rd Earls were killed fighting for the Lancastrian faction, which supported Henry IV's grandson, Henry VI, against his Yorkist rival,

Edward IV. In 1464, after the Battle of Hexham, Alnwick surrendered to John Neville, a member of the Neville family, who were the great rivals of the Percys. However, the death of Henry VI in 1471 and the exile of his queen, Margaret of Anjou, ended the wars in the North, and the 4th Earl, yet another Henry Percy, made his peace with the Yorkists. In 1483, Edward restored the Percy family to their estates. Two years later, Henry Tudor, a previously obscure descendant of the Lancastrian faction, invaded from the continent and faced Edward's successor, Richard III, at the Battle of Bosworth in Leicestershire. Henry, the 4th Earl, commanded one of Richard's divisions but stayed out of the fight while the king was surrounded and killed, thereby earning the favour of the new king, Henry VII, and his Tudor successors. The castle remained militarily important because of its position on the main Scottish invasion route, and the massive fortified gatehouse or barbican which can be seen today was finished as late as 1475. Nevertheless, early in the sixteenth century it was assessed as ineffective because of the inability of the medieval walls to resist gunpowder artillery (alnwickcastle.com). Today, the castle is open to the public and hosts numerous re-enactments and other events.

Warkworth is about 5 miles south-east of Alnwick and a mile inland from Alnmouth Bay. The castle occupies an excellent defensive position high above the River Coquet, which loops around to surround it on three sides. The first mention of a castle at Warkworth dates from around 1160, when King Henry II granted it to Roger fitz Eustace, but differing theories attribute its foundation either to David I of Scotland's son, Henry, who became Earl of Northumberland in 1139, or to Henry II himself after he regained the county from David's heir, Malcolm IV, in 1157 (see, for example, the English Heritage entry for Warkworth at english-heritage.org.uk). It seems not to have played any part in the campaign of 1174 in which William the Lion was captured. It was probably a relatively weak timber structure at this date, and may not even have been garrisoned. Earl Duncan of Fife, whom William sent to attack Warkworth (see Chapter Two), apparently met no resistance but nevertheless set fire to the town, an action which is said to have led to the deaths of 300 people who had taken refuge inside the local church (*Church Guide*, St Lawrence Warkworth, Warkworth PCC, 2011). Jordan Fantosme mentions the 'violation' of the church and the murder of the 300, but he does not specifically say that they were killed in the building, although he adds that three priests who were inside the church were castrated. English Heritage date the earliest surviving stone structures to the time of Roger's son, Robert fitz Roger, who held the castle from 1199–1214. The polygonal structure known as the Carrickfergus Tower, now ruined, is also believed to date from the early thirteenth century. The castle was besieged twice by the Scots in 1327, but it was strong enough to resist all attacks. The last descendant of Roger fitz Eustace bequeathed the castle to the crown, and in 1332 Edward III granted it to Henry, the 2nd Baron Percy, who also held Alnwick. It was largely rebuilt not long before 1400 by the 4th Baron Percy, who became the 1st Earl of Northumberland and was probably responsible for the building of the present great tower. After his son, Hotspur, was killed at Shrewsbury (see Chapter Six), the earl surrendered the castle to King Henry IV, but both Warkworth and Alnwick were restored to his grandson during the reign of Henry V. Both towns were again attacked by a Scottish army during an outbreak of hostilities in 1448 which culminated in the Battle of the River Sark (see below, Chapter Eight). During the Wars of the Roses, Warkworth was occupied by the Yorkists, but it was once again returned to the Percy family in 1471. Now a ruin, it is administered by English Heritage and is open to the public.

Bamburgh had been a stronghold of the rulers of Northumbria as long ago as the sixth century, and according to the *Anglo-Saxon Chronicle* it was first fortified by King Ida, who reigned from 547–560. Today, the castle sits on top of an outcrop of volcanic rock overlooking the sea a few miles south of Berwick, while the village of Bamburgh is a short distance inland, but in the early Anglo-Saxon era it is likely that the settlement would have been inside the fortifications. These would not have comprised a castle as we know it, but may have been no more than a wall or palisade running around the top of the rock. The *Chronicle* also tells us that Bamburgh was 'first enclosed by a stockade and thereafter by a wall', but a century after Ida the defences were evidently still made of wood, rather than earth or stone, because Bede describes how in the time of Aidan as Bishop at Lindisfarne (between 634 and 651), Bamburgh was miraculously saved from destruction at the hands of the Mercians led by the feared pagan conqueror, Penda. The invaders had driven the Northumbrian forces inside the fortification, but had failed in several attempts to capture it. Penda then ordered his men to demolish the nearby villages and pile all the wooden roof beams, rafters, wall panels and straw thatching against the town walls. They waited for a favourable westerly wind to blow from inland, then set fire to this material with the aim of burning down the defences. Bishop Aidan saw the flames while he was praying in seclusion on the nearby Farne Islands. He appealed to God to witness the 'evil' that Penda was committing, whereupon the wind changed direction and blew the flames back towards the Mercians, who were forced to abandon the siege.

The original Northumbrian defences were stormed by a Viking army during the turbulent reign of Ethelred the Unready, who ruled England from 978–1016. His reign coincided with the resumption of raids by Danish and Norwegian fleets, but the *Anglo-Saxon Chronicle* is bitterly critical of the constant delays and strategic muddle which characterized Ethelred's response. Modern scholars have tended to have a more favourable opinion of Ethelred, but the fate of Bamburgh is an illustration of the sort of frustrations that must have given contemporary chroniclers their jaundiced view. In 992, the king had ordered all the available ships to concentrate at London, with the intention of trapping the raiders in the Thames estuary, but the *Chronicle* alleges that his trusted adviser Ealdorman, Aelfric, was in league with the enemy and tipped them off. The Viking fleet thus escaped, and in the following year appeared off Northumbria and attacked Bamburgh, which 'was broken down, and much war-booty taken there'. The raiders then went on to the Humber estuary and ravaged the countryside in Yorkshire and Lincolnshire. The passage implies that the defences of Bamburgh had been completely destroyed, and we hear no more of them until after the Norman Conquest, when a castle was erected on the site. This was presumably of the usual wooden motte and bailey design, and although the precise date of its construction is not known it was definitely in existence by 1095, when it was besieged by William II during the revolt of Robert de Mowbray (see Chapter Two). After the suppression of the revolt it became a royal fortress, and English kings regularly used it as a base for their northern campaigns. The Scots besieged Bamburgh on at least three occasions – in 1138, 1328 and during the Halidon Hill campaign in 1333 – but they never succeeded in capturing it by force. On the first occasion, Eustace fitz John, who had been appointed by Henry I as Keeper of the castle, defected to the Scots, but when the Scottish army led by David I arrived to take possession, the garrison sallied out and attacked it. The Scots drove them back and even broke through the outer defences, killing around a hundred of the English, but were unable to take the keep. We know that there was a stone keep at Bamburgh by 1164, but even if the original wooden one was still in existence in 1138, it was clearly a formidable obstacle. By an agreement between David and the English King Stephen in the following year, David's son, Henry, became Earl of Northumberland, but Bamburgh Castle retained a small English garrison. The Great Hall was built in the thirteenth century by Henry III, who was also credited with introducing such comforts as glass windows. By the fifteenth century if not earlier, it had attained the form that we see today, with a massive curtain wall surrounding the central keep. The walls mainly follow the contours of the natural hill, whose steep slopes enhance their defensive strength.

Bamburgh finally fell to a besieger in 1464, but the victors were not the Scots but rather the Yorkist forces of the English King Edward IV, who had overthrown and imprisoned his predecessor, Henry VI, after the Battle of Towton in 1461. A year later, Edward occupied the castle and entrusted it to Ralph Percy, the brother of Henry, the

3rd Earl of Northumberland, who had previously been a supporter of the Lancastrian party of Henry VI but had recently gone over to Edward. However, Percy soon changed sides again and allowed Lancastrian forces into the castle under the command of Sir Ralph Grey of Heton, the Sheriff of Northumberland. In May 1464, a Yorkist army under John Neville decisively defeated the Lancastrians at the Battle of Hexham, after which the castles at Alnwick and Dunstanburgh surrendered. Grey continued to hold out, however, and on 25 June Neville laid siege to Bamburgh. He had in his train two 'great guns' named 'Newcastle' and 'London', which quickly blew the walls apart with such violence that the great stones of which they were built 'flew into the sea' (Bradbury, 1992). This is believed to be the first occasion on which an English castle was reduced by gunpowder artillery. The garrison surrendered and Grey was taken to Doncaster, where he was beheaded for treason. The castle was attacked and damaged again in 1480, when a Scottish army under the Earl of Angus mounted a brief raid into Northumberland. Bamburgh Castle today is a well-organized tourist attraction situated just north-east of the village of the same name, at grid reference NU183350. It can be reached from the A1 via the B1341 or B1342, or by taking the B1340 which runs north from Alnwick.

Chillingham, the seat of the Grey family of which the unfortunate Sir Ralph Grey of Heton was once a member, is a small village about 5 miles south-east of Wooler, near the boundary between the fertile coastal strip and the higher country inland. It is not certain when the first castle was built there. Samuel Lewis's *Topographical Dictionary of England* of 1848 states that the north-east tower dates from the reign of Henry III (1216–72), but gives no source for this assertion. However, Edward I is recorded as staying at Chillingham on his way to Scotland in 1298, at which time it was already in the possession of the Grey family, who held it until the twentieth century. Most of the present castle appears to date from the fourteenth century, and a licence to crenellate or provide it with battlements for defence, which is still on display inside, was granted by Edward III in 1344.

It was much modified in the seventeenth and eighteenth centuries, but retains its original quadrangular outline, with a massive tower at each corner. It seems to have played only a minor role in the Anglo-Scottish Wars, but in 1536 suffered considerable damage when it was besieged by rebels during the anti-Reformation uprising known as the Pilgrimage of Grace.

Today, Chillingham is best-known for its herd of white cattle, which are confined to the park but live in effect as wild animals – a unique survival of a medieval practice which was once widespread in the border regions. Although sometimes described as 'wild' cattle, they are nevertheless feral domestic animals and have no more connection than any other domestic cattle to the genuine wild ancestor of the species, the aurochs, which probably became extinct in Britain before the Roman era. The Chillingham herd is first recorded in 1645, but its association with the medieval deer park suggests that it has been there far longer. We know from medieval writers like Matthew Paris that wild cattle, presumably descended from farmyard beasts which had strayed or been abandoned, once roamed through the forests in many parts of England (Harting, 1880). According to Hector Boece, writing in 1526, the Caledonian Forest in the southern Highlands of Scotland was known for its pure white bulls, but by 1565, when Lindesay of Pitscottie wrote, they had been hunted almost to extinction because their meat was so tasty (Ritchie, 1920). So it seems quite plausible that at some point during the Norman era or later, some of these animals were driven into the newly enclosed parks with the aim of providing both food and entertainment in the form of hunting. The present owner of the castle, Sir Humphry Wakefield, has argued that a Roman oil lamp in the shape of a wild bull's head, found at Chillingham, is evidence for an association of the site with sacred cattle going back nearly 2,000 years (*The Synergy of Chillingham Cattle, Castle and Church*, in Bahn & Mutimer, eds, 2016). If we assume that the cattle were present during the medieval period, at Chillingham and perhaps elsewhere in Northumberland, they could have been a useful military resource. Harting lists several herds of similar animals which had once existed, including two in County Durham, one in Cumberland and three on the Scottish side of the border. They were presumably hunted to provide meat, like the deer with which they shared the parks, but were much more formidable quarry than deer and would not run from hounds, so they would have to be ridden down by lancers on horseback, providing their owners and guests with valuable training for war. Furthermore, as semi-wild animals they avoid people where possible, and because they were permanent residents over a long period of time they would have become 'hefted', or attached to their territory, so they could not easily be driven away by raiders like ordinary cattle. Their nervous behaviour when approached might also have made them useful by giving warning of the proximity of enemy raiding parties (Wakefield, *op. cit.*).

Chillingham Castle (grid reference NU061258) has been continuously occupied since the fourteenth century and still gives a good impression of a medieval stronghold. Apart from the cattle, its fame rests mainly on its claim to be the 'most haunted castle in England', and it has to be said that it looks the part. It can be reached by minor roads from either Alnwick or Wooler; there are occasional buses from both towns to the village. The castle is open to visitors from late March until November. The wild cattle can be observed only on guided tours, which are best booked in advance. The little church of Saint Peter just north of the castle (grid reference NU062259) is well known locally for the spectacular tomb of Sir Ralph Grey I and his wife, Lady Elizabeth, who died in 1442 and 1445 respectively. The effigies on the tomb are of expensive alabaster, which had to be imported all the way from south Derbyshire, and the whole edifice seems far too elaborate for its humble setting. One possible explanation is suggested by the fact that that the tomb was commissioned by the couple's son, the same Sir Ralph who was executed after the fall of Bamburgh (see above). It may have been intended for a more suitable location, perhaps in a great cathedral, but after Sir Ralph junior's fall from grace the family thought it wiser to keep it in the obscurity of a small country church (Philip Deakin, 'The Church of St Peter, Chillingham', in Bahn & Mutimer, 2016).

Other prominent features in the counties on both sides of the border are the lesser fortifications known as Pele (or Peel) towers, Tower houses and Bastle houses. The terminology is often used imprecisely and it is not always easy to differentiate between the three types of building. The Gatehouse website gazetteer of medieval fortifications in England and Wales treats both Tower houses and Peles as part of a continuum, with the larger stone-built Tower houses belonging to higher-status families and the smaller Peles being more associated with the lesser gentry (gatehouse-gazeteer.info/Indexs/EngCounty/EPT.html). Some edifices, like Cocklaw Tower at Wall, near Hexham, are classified as both Pele towers and fortified manor houses. A Tower house is basically a fortified house in the form of a freestanding rectangular stone tower, in essence a keep without the surrounding curtain walls. By the fifteenth century, this design had become the norm even for larger private castles in Scotland, where few of the aristocracy attained the wealth or the independence of their English counterparts (Reid, 2006). Keith Durham (2008), however, distinguishes the stone Tower house from the Pele, which was made from thick oak trunks and surrounded by wooden palisade. He describes a typical Tower house as four or five storeys high, with battlemented walls and a solidly built basement, the whole structure reaching from 40–60 feet in height. Many if not all such towers originally had attached halls and other unfortified structures attached to them, but these have seldom survived (King, 2007). Entry to the tower itself was intentionally made difficult to enable a handful of occupants to fight off more numerous attackers, with the only access being via a small wooden door and an inner iron gate at ground level, a spiral staircase in one corner leading to the upper floors.

A Bastle is a two-storey house of more normal proportions, distinguished by very thick walls but otherwise outwardly similar to any other stone farmhouse. The occupants lived on the first floor, with the ground floor used for livestock and storage of goods. The entrance to the upper storey was situated high up on the wall and could be reached only by a ladder, which was designed to be pulled up to prevent an enemy from breaking down the door. All of these designs were used as dwelling houses as well as for defence against raiders, and between the fourteenth and sixteenth centuries they became increasingly popular with border families of moderate means. Also common in many border parishes were fortified churches, which could provide refuges for the poorer members of their congregations, who typically lived in smaller and more vulnerable cottages. Even the church on the island of Lindisfarne, which was the home of a Benedictine priory from the thirteenth to the sixteenth centuries, was fortified with battlements and loops for crossbowmen to shoot through, although it never seems to have been attacked (Tristram, 2009). Alternatively, a Pele tower might be built near to the village church. Today, these are often known as 'Vicars' Peles', because their handy location led to many being converted into vicarages once their defensive role had become obsolete. The Gatehouse website lists more than eighty Peles, Tower houses and Bastle houses in Northumberland alone, excluding those whose dating is uncertain or of which no visible masonry survives. The most famous survivor is probably the tower at Smailholm, near Kelso on the Scottish side of the border, but intact tower houses in Northumberland include Embleton near Dunstanburgh (grid reference NU230224) and Preston, north of Alnwick (NU183254). Not all of them are open to the casual visitor and some are private homes, but the tower at Whittingham, west of Alnwick (grid reference NU069118), after a career as a Victorian alms house, has recently been repurposed as holiday accommodation. The Vicar's Pele in Corbridge, near Hexham (grid reference NY987644), has undergone another change of use in keeping with the times, and is now a brewery and public house.

Chapter Eight

'The English by Guile Won the Day': The Road to Flodden, 1513

Date	9 September 1513
Location	Branxton, Northumberland
Combatants	Scots under King James IV versus English under Thomas Howard, Earl of Surrey
Outcome	English victory

THE HUNDRED YEARS' War with France that Edward III had begun so successfully with his victory at Crecy finally ended in defeat for the English at the hands of a resurgent French army, aided on several occasions by their Scottish allies. The last major English possession in the country, Bordeaux, was lost after the Battle of Castillon in 1453, and the war was formally ended in 1475 by the Treaty of Picquigny. By that time, England had already been embroiled for a decade in the power struggle which later became known as the Wars of the Roses, which only ended in 1485 with the victory of the Tudor dynasty under Henry VII. The new English king was less interested in further military adventures than in putting his country and its finances on a stable footing after the decades of war, and at first his relations with his northern neighbour seemed to have taken a permanent turn for the better. The Scottish King James IV ascended the throne three years later. He was the sixth ruler of the House of Stewart, which had begun with Robert II more than a century earlier. Since that time, the Scottish monarchy had continued to be dogged by poor management and bad luck. Robert III died in February 1406, by which time his 11-year-old son, who now became James I, had already been captured by English pirates while en route to supposed safety in France, and handed over to Henry IV of England. He was not released until 1424, when Henry's son, the warlike Henry V, died. The latter's successor, Henry VI, was an infant and his council was anxious for peace, so James was allowed to return to Scotland. He attempted to revive his predecessors' assertive policy towards his southern neighbour, but without much success. In 1436, he renewed the French alliance and attacked the English garrison in Roxburgh Castle, but retreated when a relief army approached, abandoning his artillery. The debacle exacerbated the discontent which was already growing in the kingdom, and James was murdered in February 1437. His queen, Joan Beaufort, and his young son, James, escaped and later took a terrible revenge on the assassins. James II was only 6 years old when he came to the throne, but he grew up to be a popular ruler with a keen interest in military affairs. In 1448, a fresh outbreak of war with England saw tit-for-tat attacks on Alnwick, Warkworth, Dunbar and Dumfries, followed by an invasion of Scotland by Hotspur's son, Henry Percy, 2nd Earl of Northumberland (Rose, 2002). Percy advanced by the west coast route and was brought to battle by a Scottish army led by Hugh Douglas, the Earl of Ormonde, on the banks of the tidal River Sark near Gretna. Percy deployed his archers as his father had done at Homildon Hill, but this time the Scottish spearmen charged without delay and the open terrain provided no obstacles behind which the archers could take cover. Lindesay of Pitscottie (1814) tells us that the English were routed in the first clash and driven into the river, suffering heavy casualties. This often-neglected battle shows that the Scottish tactic of seeking close combat to neutralize the enemy archery still remained viable, sixty years after its last great success at Otterburn.

In 1460, James II followed his father in laying siege to Roxburgh Castle, this time with the aid of a train of new and powerful cannon. On 3 August, he was watching his guns in action when one of them exploded. Lindesay of Pitscottie says that a piece of the barrel struck him on the thigh and broke it, a wound which quickly proved fatal.

Yet again, a monarch's premature death meant that the new king, his son, James III, was only a child, but even when he attained his majority this James proved to be an unpopular ruler, and he had to contend with several attempts to overthrow him. On 11 June 1488, he was defeated by rebels led by the earls of Hume, Bothwell and Angus at the Battle of Sauchieburn near Stirling, and was either killed in the fighting or murdered shortly afterwards. According to Lindesay of Pitscottie, it was the attack of the men of Annandale that put James to flight and decided the battle; George Buchanan adds the interesting detail that this was because they carried longer spears than their opponents. Pitscottie claims that one of his own ancestors gave the king a grey horse that was said to be faster than any other, but it threw him and left him to be overtaken by the rebels. The victors placed the late king's son, James IV, on the throne, but this James, who at 15 years old was relatively mature for a Scottish king in this period, was a very different character from his father.

James IV played an active role in the government of his realm from the start, and was largely successful in neutralizing the problems which he had inherited from his ineffectual predecessor. As early as 1489, he crushed a dangerous rebellion by the Earl of Lennox and the Master of Huntly. He also took on the MacDonald Lords of the Isles, who had in practice been independent rulers since the reign of Robert II, and forced them to acknowledge his overlordship. He went on to put the crown's finances on a more stable footing with the acquisition of the revenues of the Archbishopric of Saint Andrews, to which he contrived to appoint a succession of his relatives. Much of the money went on the armed forces, especially the navy and the artillery train, which were greatly strengthened. James pursued an active foreign policy, and in 1492 he renewed the 'Auld Alliance' with France. He granted asylum to Perkin Warbeck, an adventurer who claimed to be the Duke of York, one of the princes said to have been murdered in the Tower of London by Richard III, and in 1496 he invaded Northumbria in support of Warbeck's claim to the English throne. When the expected local support failed to materialize, he withdrew. In a dramatic change of policy towards England, James turned to diplomacy, and in 1502 he signed a Treaty of Perpetual Peace with Henry VII, in which both monarchs agreed not only never again to go to war with each other, but to bind their successors to the same terms. The treaty was guaranteed by the Pope, who undertook to excommunicate any party who broke it. This was the first formal peace treaty between England and Scotland since 1328, as opposed to the usual temporary truces, and the agreement was sealed with James's marriage to Henry's eldest daughter, Margaret Tudor. It was, of course, incompatible with the terms of the Auld Alliance with France, and if England and France went to war again it would place James in a difficult position. But ultimately it was the attitude of the English King Henry VIII, who succeeded his father in 1509, that ensured that the French alliance would prevail.

Despite its sinister role in the history of Scotland, the Flodden campaign can be seen as a mere sideshow in the longstanding rivalry between the Holy Roman Empire and the Kingdom of France, which had been principally fought out in Italy since the French had invaded that country in 1494. In 1511, Pope Julius II proclaimed a Holy League against France, in which the Papal States and the Emperor Maximilian I were joined by Spain, Venice and the Swiss Confederacy. Henry VIII of England also threw in his lot with the League, and in May 1513 he invaded France. King Louis XII of France responded by invoking his country's historic alliance with Scotland, according to which each agreed to help the other if they were attacked. Henry had inherited a peaceful kingdom and a full treasury, but he was naturally more warlike than his father had been, and more ambitious when it came to increasing the power and prestige of both his kingdom and himself. His view was that the treaty of 1502 had not altered the traditional relationship between the two realms, which – in England at least – had always been assumed to imply the overlordship of the English monarch and the subservience of his Scottish counterpart. James needed to be put in his place, and in 1512 a diplomatic offensive was launched to do just that. First, the English parliament passed the Subsidy Act, which openly referred to the 'homage and obedience' owed to Henry by the Scots, and then the Archbishop of York persuaded Pope Julius to excommunicate James on the grounds that he had broken the Treaty of Perpetual Peace. At that time he had not in fact done so, although he had invited French advisors to help update his army, introducing improved artillery and re-equipping his infantry with longer pikes in the continental style. This was the Scottish king's real offence, of course; simply to maintain good relations with France, the enemy of the Holy League. But having already paid the penalty of excommunication, he now had nothing to lose by openly joining the French side, and in May 1513, when Henry embarked on his expedition across the Channel, James also began making preparations for war. Henry ignored James's demands that he halt operations against the French, and retaliated by accusing his rival of mistreating his sister, Margaret. On 25 July, a Scottish fleet put to sea under the command of James Hamilton, the Earl of Arran. Sailing around the north of Scotland, it sacked the English-held town of Carrickfergus in Ireland before joining the French fleet at Brest, probably with the aim of cutting off Henry's lines of communication across the English Channel.

Anticipating the international condemnation that he would receive for being the first to resort to arms, James still needed a pretext if he was actually to invade England, but one was conveniently provided by an illegitimate son of a prominent Northumberland family, the Herons of Ford and Thornton. John, the so-called 'bastard Heron', was wanted in Scotland for the murder of Robert Kerr, the Warden of the Scottish Middle March, and had taken refuge in England. Since Kerr's death in 1508, James had repeatedly asked for Heron to be handed over for trial, but nothing had been done. On 5 August, Alexander, 3rd Lord Hume, led an advanced guard of 7,000 Scottish Border horse to ravage Northumberland. However, on the 13th they were ambushed and routed by English archers under Sir William Bulmer on Millfield Plain, only 2 miles north-west of the ill-omened battlefield of Homildon Hill. Hume escaped, but he lost 1,000 of his men and all his booty in what came to be known to the Scots as the 'Ill Raid'. Only three days later, Henry and the Emperor Maximilian defeated a smaller French force outside Therouanne, near Calais, in a clash which would become famous as the Battle of the Spurs, from the speed with which the French cavalry fled the scene. James's senior herald, Sir William Cumming, the Lyon King of Arms, had already delivered an ultimatum to Henry, warning him that unless he at once desisted from attacking James's 'brother and cousin', Louis, the Scots would do whatever was necessary to compel him. Naturally, Henry ignored the demand. So James gathered his army at Edinburgh during the third week of August, and on the 20th he began the march towards the border, picking up the Borderer contingents at Ellemford. This site, a large area of open ground near a ford across the Whiteadder Water about 6 miles north-east of Duns, was a traditional muster point for Scottish armies preparing to cross the border. There was a chapel there, known as Ellem Kirk, where James offered prayers for the success of the expedition. Then on the 22nd, the largest Scottish invasion force ever sent against England crossed the Tweed at the ford near Coldstream and marched into Northumbria, under the personal command of the king.

The Armies

The exact strength of James's army is not known. Two English sources, Edward Hall and the author of the near-contemporary document entitled *The Trewe Encountre or Batayl Lately Don Between Englande and Scotlande*, give a figure of 100,000 men, and Thomas Howard, reporting after the battle, claimed an almost equally implausible 80,000. By contrast, the Scots tended to err on the low side, with Lindesay of Pitscottie quoting 30,000 and George Buchanan half that figure. (The relevant extract from Hall's *Triumphant Reigne of Kyng Henry the VIII* is quoted in Barr, 2001, Appendix V. See also Laing, 1867. Barr also quotes extracts from the *Trewe Encountre*, Lord Thomas Howard's own dispatch and the account of Lindesay of Pitscottie.) We might assume that Scottish writers would have had better access to reliable information, but of course it was common practice to exaggerate enemy numbers while minimizing your own, in order to excuse a defeat or make a victory seem more heroic. John Sadler (2006) gives a detailed order of battle which adds up to a total of 42,000 men, and although this may be a reliable tally of the numbers originally raised for the campaign, attrition and the provision of detachments might account for the discrepancy between that figure and Pitscottie's. Not only was this the biggest Scottish army ever sent against England, it was also the most up to date. James had assembled a train of heavy artillery, equipped the Lowland spearmen with the new 18ft pikes which were in vogue in Europe and ensured that as many of his men as possible were protected by plate armour. The nobility were not deployed separately from the common spearmen, as had been the traditional practice, but were expected to fight in their front ranks with the same weapons. Fergus Cannan (2009) implies that one of the causes of the Scottish defeat at Flodden was that the old 'tried and tested' 12ft spear had been replaced by these longer and more unwieldy pikes, which the Scottish infantry were not trained to use. David Caldwell (quoted in Scott, 2023) has suggested that James's experience at the Battle of Sauchieburn, where the long spears of the Annandale men are said to have given them a decisive edge, may have influenced the king's choice of weapons. However, as Jenn Scott points out, a length of 6 ells (5.6 metres, or just over 18ft) had been prescribed by an Act of Parliament as early as 1471, although ten years later this had been slightly reduced to 'at least' 5 ells. The Scots had therefore had forty years to familiarize themselves with pikes of this sort of length, and in doing so they were following the example of the most successful infantry in Europe, the Swiss, who had replaced their traditional halberds with similar pikes following a defeat at the Battle of Arbedo in 1422 (Heath, 1982). Jonathan Cooper (2008) has pointed out that there were Scots serving in the French Army at this time, and they would have seen European armies in action at battles such as Fornovo (1495) and Ravenna (1512). It should be noted, however, that the Acts of Parliament of 1471 and 1481 did not state that every man must have a long spear, merely that there should be no short ones, and that everyone who did not possess a spear or a bow must have a 'good axe and a targe of leather to resist the shot of England' (Scott).

This implies that at that time the Scots still did not operate in the sort of homogenous formations which would have been needed to achieve the full effect of the Swiss tactics. The Swiss had a system of selective conscription that enabled the young and unmarried men to devote much of their time to mustering and drilling, and their 'keils', as the deep pike formations were called, could manoeuvre at speed over difficult ground and change their facing to ward off threats to their flanks while still maintaining the close order necessary for mutual support (Predonanzi & Alberici, 2021). The mercenary German Landsknechts who copied them were paid professionals who could achieve similar levels of expertise, but the kings of Scots never succeeded in persuading their part-time levies to do likewise. Forty French officers led by the Sieur d'Aussi had arrived in Scotland at the end of July 1513 to train the men in the art of using the pike, but they had less than a month to do so before the invasion began, which was nowhere near enough time to achieve useful results.

Pikes could easily outreach any opponent so long as the men wielding them advanced close enough together to support each other and present an unbroken row of spearheads, but without this mutual support their users would be helpless against an enemy who could slip past their points and attack from close range with a shorter weapon. Therefore, as soon as a formation of pikemen was disrupted and the melee broke down into a series of individual combats, a more flexible opponent armed with handier weapons would have the advantage. It is also important to realize that by the time of Flodden, even the Swiss pike tactics were no longer at the cutting edge, as their opponents were developing new battlefield methods to counter them, including field defences and massed artillery. The Battle of Novara, which was fought against the French in Italy in June 1513, was in fact the last great victory of the Swiss pikes, and it was achieved only by a surprise dawn attack on the encircled French camp. Two years later, at Marignano, the French cavalry and artillery finally stopped the keils, inflicting on them such heavy losses that the Swiss never again took the field as an independent force.

Not everyone in James's army was equipped with the new weapons. It seems that the infantry recruited from the Borders did carry pikes, but their mounted comrades served as light cavalry. It is a testimony to the success of his attempts at nation-building that, turbulent though the Highlands still were – it was only twenty years since the Lords of the Isles had been brought to heel – nearly all of the clans sent contingents, led by their chiefs or their close relatives, to serve in the royal army. Even deadly enemies like the MacDonalds and the Campbells were obliged to put aside their differences and march side-by-side. By this time, however, the Highland and Lowland Scots had grown apart, not only in language and culture but in their styles of fighting. The clansmen of the north and west were never re-equipped as pikemen, but continued to fight with their traditional bows, two-handed swords and axes. Instead of plate armour, they preferred coats of mail and pointed, open-faced bascinet helmets of distinctly old-fashioned appearance. In part, perhaps, this stemmed from cultural conservatism, but it also reflected a preference for speed of movement, especially in difficult terrain. In these respects, the Highland warriors resembled the halberdiers or sword and buckler men who accompanied the pikemen in some continental armies, using their mobility to guard the flanks of the unwieldy pike blocks and disrupt the enemy's formations. Unfortunately, however, there seems to be no evidence that they were intentionally deployed in this role in the Scottish army, but rather they were placed in separate units on the wings of the army, where many found themselves far from the decisive point at the climax of the battle.

In the absence of King Henry, who was campaigning in France, his wife, Katherine of Aragon, was acting as regent in England, and she reacted decisively to the invasion, dispatching an army about 26,000 strong (Sadler, 2006), raised mainly from the North and Midlands, and led by the veteran soldier Thomas Howard, Earl of Surrey. The earl was now 70 years old and had begun his military career fighting for Edward IV at the Battle of Barnet in 1471. His continued support for the Yorkists had earned him three years in prison after Henry VII took the throne, but he was eventually released after arguing that he had always been loyal to the crowned king, whoever he was, and that he could be relied on to fight for Henry just as he had done for his predecessors. In the 1490s, Surrey served as the king's lieutenant in the North, where he dealt successfully with several rebellions and Scottish incursions. In 1503, he accompanied Princess Margaret to Scotland, where she was to be married to James IV, and the Scottish king and English earl quickly became good friends. When Henry VIII came to the throne, however, Surrey found himself outmanoeuvred by the king's favourite, Thomas Wolsey, and fell out of favour. It was for this reason that he had been left behind to guard the Scottish frontier instead of accompanying the king to France.

Henry was not oblivious to the recent developments in European warfare, and for his expedition to France he had hired a contingent of German Landsknechts, pikemen who fought in the Swiss style with the same 18ft weapons as the Scots were bringing to Flodden. But he considered the Scottish front to be a sideshow, and the men left behind to hold it were still armed with their traditional bows, though increasingly stiffened by men equipped for hand-to-hand combat with a type of polearm known as a bill. Niall Barr (2001) might be overstating the case when he describes the northern levies as 'second rate'; they practised diligently with their weapons and would soon prove how effectively they could wield them. But from a tactical point of view, they would have more closely resembled James's Highlanders than his reformed pikemen, although the English, like the Lowland Scots, preferred reinforced jacks and plate armour to mail. However, the tactical role of the billmen was quite different, because in the absence of their own pikemen they formed the main close-quarters fighting force of the army, and on them would fall the responsibility of facing the Scottish pikes in battle. Their weapon, the English bill, must by European standards have seemed very much an anachronism by 1513. In fact, it was a very similar weapon to the halberds that the Swiss had once used, but had abandoned in favour of the pike after 1422. In origin, the bill was a hedging tool, resembling a small scythe blade on a wooden shaft, but at some point during the early fifteenth century it was transformed into a weapon by the addition of a point on the end, and often also a spike on the back of the blade. The length of the shaft varied from 5–8ft, which made it a handier weapon than the pike in a confused hand-to-hand fight, but it maintained an advantage in reach over shorter weapons like the sword and one-handed axe. It was wielded in two hands, and so combined the cutting power of an axe with the thrusting ability of a spear. Reese (2003) points out that the technique for wielding a bill against a human target was very similar to that for cutting a hedge, so it would have come naturally to most countrymen, in contrast to the complex and counterintuitive drills required of the Scottish pikemen. It is often stated that the bills could actually cut through the shafts of an enemy's pikes, which is admittedly what Bishop Ruthal of Durham seems to suggest when he says that they 'disappointed the Scots of the long spears wherein was their greatest trust' (quoted in Strickland & Hardy, 2005), but it seems unlikely that this would be a common occurrence. A pike staff was usually protected by langets, strips of metal extending perhaps one or two feet down from the head, which were devised precisely to prevent this happening. And an 18ft wooden shaft held at one end would in any case have enough flexibility to be knocked down, rather than cut through, by any but the very sharpest of edges. But a heavy blade like that of a bill would be very effective at knocking aside longer weapons, and the wielder could then step forward and deliver a crushing blow to his temporarily vulnerable opponent, which might knock him down even if it failed to penetrate his armour. Billmen first appeared as a distinct troop type in English armies around the middle of the fifteenth century

(Heath, 1982), and during the Wars of the Roses they became one of the mainstays of the infantry forces, along with the archers. Their rise was probably a response to the increasing effectiveness of plate armour, which was difficult to penetrate with arrows. As the use of a shield in combination with a two-handed weapon was impossible, the billmen usually wore substantial body armour themselves, often including a helmet and a cuirass of steel plate.

By this time, gunpowder artillery was beginning to play a significant role on the battlefield, but the two sides had employed very different approaches to its use. The Scottish kings had continued to strengthen and modernize their heavy siege cannons, despite James II's unfortunate mishap at Roxburgh Castle. Medieval guns were usually made from staves of iron welded together and strengthened by iron hoops which were shrunk on to hold them firmly in place. The process was similar to that for making wooden barrels, hence the name given to the tube of a gun. By 1500, however, heavy guns were also being cast in one piece from bronze. These, like the largest iron guns, were loaded through the muzzle, but the breeches of some of the small iron pieces could be unscrewed to enable them to be loaded from that end. In theory, the larger guns could fire projectiles to greater ranges, but this advantage was of little value in a field engagement because their accuracy was so poor, and techniques for estimating range and allowing for the curved trajectory of the shot were rudimentary. The usual missiles were solid balls of stone or iron, optimized for knocking down stone fortifications, but large numbers of small shot could be loaded to give a shotgun effect against personnel at close range. The largest cannon ever fielded in Britain was the famous Mons Meg, now restored and on display in Edinburgh Castle, which was cast in the traditional way from iron staves, has a calibre of 20in (510mm) and fired a ball weighing 386lb (175kg). This gun, one of the biggest in Europe, was a gift to James II from the Duke of Burgundy and saw action in several sieges, including that of Norham in 1497, but its great weight made it difficult to move overland and it was not taken on the Flodden campaign. The guns that did accompany

James's army, though, comprised a very powerful force. According to the Treasurer's Accounts, the Scottish train included five heavy guns firing 60lb balls (60-pdrs), two 18-pdrs, four 6-pdrs and several lighter pieces (Sadler & Serdiville). They were commanded by the royal artillery master, Robert Borthwick, who may have cast the heavier cannon himself in the newly established foundries at Stirling and Edinburgh. By contrast, the English gun founding industry was still rudimentary, and although Surrey brought with him twenty-two guns he had nothing larger than a 6-pdr, most of them being 2-pdr 'falcons'. But the lightness of the English artillery was not the disadvantage that it might have seemed, because the smaller breech loaders could be loaded and fired much faster than muzzle loaders. Sadler & Serdiville (2013) suggest that the heavy Scottish artillery could fire about one shot per minute, and the lighter English pieces 'twice or even three times that'.

The Invasion

After crossing the Tweed, James marched the 7 miles downstream to Norham, and on the following day laid siege to the castle there, supported by his heavy guns firing from the north bank of the river. The section of wall facing the river was soon breached, but the garrison nevertheless managed to beat off a series of assaults over the next few days. At last, on 29 August, having run out of powder and shot and seeing no prospect of relief, they were forced to surrender. The Scottish army then advanced southwards up the valley of the River Till, which runs into the Tweed from the south near Twizell Bridge, halfway between Coldstream and Norham. On the way they took the castles at Etal and Ford with little resistance. Ford, the stronghold of the Heron family, had been left under the command of the Lady Heron, as her husband was already a prisoner of the Scots. She had appealed to the Earl of Surrey for help, but had been informed that the English army was still too far away to intervene. A story which apparently originated with Robert Lindesay of Pitscottie has it that James and the Lady Heron subsequently embarked on a romantic affair, as a result of which the king delayed longer than necessary at Ford instead of marching south to seek out the English army. James was a notorious womanizer who earned the disapproval of the austere Lindesay, who adds that he had been warned by a seer before the campaign to 'meddle with no women', or else he would be brought to ruin. (It is an interesting comment on the king's superstitious nature that George Buchanan claims that the man was an actor hired by the queen, who was opposed to the war as well as to her husband's infidelities, and considered him gullible enough to be influenced by such a trick.) On the other hand, as John Sadler points out, he burnt Ford when he finally left, which would have been an uncharacteristically unchivalrous act if the rumours had been true. A more likely reason for the delay was the weather, which was unseasonably wet, windy and cold. This added to the risk of disease as well as making the movement of the heavy artillery on muddy roads even more difficult than usual. What is more, merely by marching his army into England, James had already achieved his principal objective, which was to divert English attention from the war in France. Naturally, he would have been very happy to win a major battle, which would set the seal on his international reputation as a Renaissance prince and perhaps impress the more recalcitrant elements in his own country. But it was not necessary to push deeper into hostile territory in order to achieve this, as he was confident that the English would rise to the bait and come north to meet him.

He was right. Documents which survive in the National Archives in London show that Queen Katherine was very active in supporting a counteroffensive in the North (Cunningham, 2020). She arranged for 1,500 'Almain rivets' or suits of German plate armour to be collected, together with additional 'ordnance' (artillery), and personally took them north as far as Warwick. She also ordered Sir Thomas Lovell to raise an army in the Midlands in case the Scots should defeat or bypass the Earl of Surrey's forces in the North. Surrey was at

Pontefract in Yorkshire when he learned of the Scottish invasion and did not start to put his plans in motion until three days after James had crossed the Tweed, but then he too moved decisively. On 30 August, he arrived at Newcastle, the muster point which had been designated for the English army, and the troops began to assemble there two days later. James did not leave Ford until 5 September, by which time Surrey was already at Bolton in Glendale near Alnwick, less than 20 miles away. But the Scottish king did not retire to safety, claiming to have completed his mission, as Surrey probably expected. Instead he marched to Flodden Edge, 2 miles south-west of Ford, where he arrayed his army along the ridge and prepared for battle. The biggest and bloodiest of all the battles fought between the English and the Scots would take place just a couple of miles south of the border near the little Northumberland village of Branxton, but it has become known to history not by the name of the place where it happened but by the place where the Scots had intended to fight: near the even smaller village of Flodden. It seems that although James had no intention of retreating, he was keen to maximize his advantages. His army seemed to be both more numerous and better equipped than the English, its artillery was better and its new position was a very strong one, which Surrey could hardly hope to attack successfully. Flodden Edge is a continuation of the same feature on which stands Homildon Hill, only 5 miles to the south-east. Like the latter it overlooks the River Till and the flat coastal plain beyond, and the top of the ridge commands the only feasible approach from the south-east. To attack by this route would have required Surrey's men to ascend a long slope, devoid of trees or any other kind of cover, in full view of the emplaced Scottish guns on the top. It was in this position that Surrey's herald, Rouge Croix, found King James and issued his master's challenge to battle. James briefly detained Rouge Croix in custody to prevent him returning with details of the Scottish deployment, and sent his own emissary, the Islay Herald, to accept the challenge. But when Surrey arrived within sight of Flodden Edge and debriefed his messenger, he quickly realized that the enemy's position was impregnable. Rouge Croix was sent back with another message, this time reproaching James for digging-in in a defensive position while pretending to be willing to fight, and summoning him to bring his army down onto the level ground on the following day, 8 September, so that the issue could be decided in a fair encounter in the open. Not surprisingly, James refused to be drawn into throwing away his advantage, and impatiently replied that it was not fitting for a king to obey orders from a mere earl. Niall Barr (2001) concludes that despite his efforts to modernize his army, James was well aware that it would be at a disadvantage against the English in a battle in the open, hence his reluctance to abandon his defensive position.

Clearly, Surrey was not going to be able to move the Scots by argument, so it was decided that the English should instead attempt to outmanoeuvre them. Exactly who first had the idea has been frequently debated. The often repeated story that it came from the Bastard Heron has been described by John Sadler (2006) as a 'legend', but Heron would have had the necessary local knowledge and is known to have been with the army as he performed with distinction in the forthcoming battle. On the morning of 8 September, the English army struck its camp at Wooler and embarked on a march around the Scots with the aim of cutting their lines of communication, thus forcing James to abandon the Flodden position. As Sadler points out, for the first few miles of the northward leg of the march they would have been visible from the Scottish lines, but when they passed behind the high ground known as Watch Hill or Watch Law, which rises out of the plain a mile-and-a-half north-east of Ford, James and his advisors must have been in a state of uncertainty about their intentions. Why the Scottish border horsemen were not sent out at once to shadow the enemy and report on their movements is not clear, although there may have been suspicions about their loyalty, which the experience of the battle on the following day would partly justify. Surrey could easily have continued on to Berwick and garrisoned the town, or even have crossed the border and ravaged the lands of the Marcher lords on the other side. But on the following morning, 9 September, he instead turned east and marched north of Watch Law towards the village of Duddo, north of Etal, and the crossings of the River Till, thus threatening the Scottish rear. The advance guard probably reached Twizell Bridge, which spans the Till just above its confluence with the Tweed, not long before noon. It would have been difficult to get 26,000 men across the narrow bridge in much less than a day, but most of the army probably had to give priority to the guns and wagons and wade the stream. The weather was cold and wet and they were short of food, but according to the *Trewe Encountre* they responded enthusiastically to a morale-boosting speech from Surrey, who exhorted them to fight 'like Englishmen'.

When the English manoeuvre was finally spotted and reported to James, he realized that his position on top of Flodden Edge was now untenable, but he refused his council's advice to fall back across the Tweed, arguing that it would be dishonourable to retreat. This would have been more dangerous than fighting, as the enemy were now across his lines of communication. The only other option was to about-face and take up a new position further north, and a suitable location appeared to exist about a mile nearer to the border, on another parallel ridge, Branxton Hill, which overlooked the village of that name and the slightly lower height of Piper Hill to the north. It was here, on the afternoon of 9 September 1513, that the battle was fought. The terrain on Branxton Hill was probably mostly open rough grazing, with an extensive strip of marshy ground at its base, between it and Piper Hill, which was to prove a significant factor in the fight. The Historic England battlefield report suggests that, although there is no surviving trace of sixteenth-century arable farming here, at least some of the lower ground in the vicinity of Branxton village would have been unenclosed ridge and furrow planted with cereal crops. We do not know whether they would already have been harvested at the time of the battle, but the undulating ground, whether it was covered with standing crops or merely stubble, would have been an additional factor in slowing the advance of the Scots. The two armies now deployed, with three of the four main English divisions or 'battles' drawn up on Piper Hill; from right to left these were the divisions of Edmund Howard, Thomas Howard, the Lord Admiral, and their father, the Earl of Surrey. The latter was only just deploying into position when the battle began, causing some alarm to the Lord Admiral, who sent an urgent message to his father asking for assistance. A small force of mounted men, under Lord Dacre, was drawn up to the rear of Edmund Howard's division. The fourth division, that of Sir Edward Stanley, had been the last to leave camp and was still more than an hour's march away behind the English left flank. Opposite them, two solid pike blocks were formed in the Scottish centre; the larger on the right was led by the king himself and faced his opposite number, the Earl of Surrey, with the division under the earls of Errol, Crawford and Montrose deployed on his left. On the far left of the line were Lord Hume's Borderers, supported by Gordons and other clansmen from the central Highlands led by Alexander Gordon, the Earl of Huntly. A small reserve division led by the Earl of Bothwell was drawn up behind the king's position, while on James's right were the remainder of the Highland contingents – Campbells, MacDonalds, Mackenzies and MacLeans from the west coast, Mackays from the far north and other smaller clans, all commanded by the earls of Lennox and Argyll.

As the armies began to move, the artillery of both sides opened fire, but despite the greater weight of the Scottish guns they failed to do as much damage as James must have expected. Not only did they shoot more slowly than the English guns, but in their new location they had not been sited as carefully as they had been on Flodden Edge, and could not command the same field of fire. Bishop Leslie of Ross says that the English artillerymen 'shot fast and did great scathe', and attributes the ineffectiveness of their Scottish opposite numbers to the fact that, being deployed along the top of the ridge, they 'shot over the English army' as it descended the slope of Piper Hill. John Sadler rightly points out that this failure cannot have been because the guns could not be depressed far enough to fire at targets on lower ground, because this could easily have been done by placing wedges under the carriages or digging in the front wheels, which must have been the plan in any case when siting them to defend the Flodden Edge position. Perhaps there was not time to do this before the battle began, and the Scottish gunners simply lost their heads under the pressure of trying to remedy the omission while already under fire themselves. Many of them were relatively inexperienced, as the best artillerymen had been allocated to serve with the fleet. With the two sides within sight of each other at a distance of less than half a mile, the longer range of the big guns was now irrelevant, as the small English pieces were just as effective at ranges up to about 600 yards (Strickland & Hardy, 2005). Both Barr (2003) and Sadler suggest that one reason for the poor showing of the heavy balls fired by the Scots was that when they landed on the soft wet ground they sank into the mud rather than ricocheting, but this implies that they fell short of the English line rather than overshooting, as Leslie specifically says. According to Edward Hall, the English began with counterbattery fire against the Scottish guns, which 'slew the master gunner of Scotland and beat all his men from the field'. We know that Borthwick was not actually killed, but his guns must soon have ceased firing because Hall goes on to tell us that the English pieces then switched their fire onto the schiltrons of the king's own division and caused many casualties. One stray cannon ball, however, landed close enough to some of Lord Dacre's English Border horse on the right wing to persuade them to retire temporarily, which was unfortunate for Surrey's men because it was on that wing that the first of the enemy's blows fell.

Dacre's own report implied that the guns did not fire until the battle had already been joined on the Scottish left, but most modern commentators agree that it was the failure of his artillery that persuaded James to order a general advance, which is what the *Trewe Encountre* specifically says: 'our gonnes did soe break and constreyn the Scottissh great army, that some parte of thaim wer enforsed to come doun the said hilles'(Laing, 1867; see also Sadler & Serdiville, pp.150 –52). If the Scottish guns had outshot their opposite numbers and begun to target the enemy's main line of battle, as the king must have expected, it would have been Surrey who would have been forced to attack or leave his men standing in the open to be shot down. But Surrey was only getting into position at this point, and the Scottish advance left his son's division still looking dangerously exposed. At about 4.00 pm, the Scottish left wing opened the battle by charging down the hill, which was relatively gentle in that sector, into the English position opposite them. These Scots possessed two advantages that their main body and right wing did not have: the valley between the two hills was more shallow here than in the Scottish centre, and the marshy ground at the bottom was less extensive. Hume's Borderers also had the support of the more mobile Highlanders, with their swords and bows, who could guard their comrades' flanks and intervene against the flanks of the enemy when the main bodies clashed. In fact, Huntly's Highlanders were not just supporting troops for the pikemen, but proved themselves capable of engaging the English billmen frontally and defeating them. The Gordons crashed into the English line frontally and drove them back. Hall alleged that many of the Cheshire and Lancashire levies were unenthusiastic and fled before the Scots reached them, but others must have stood firm because a number of knights from both counties were listed among the dead. According to one account, the impact of the levelled pikes 'put many over, that the blood ran out burst at their broken harness' (Sadler & Serdiville), while Pitscottie tells how the Highlanders 'witht their bowis and tua handit swords wrocht sa manfullie' that they defeated the Englishmen facing them with no loss to themselves. Edmund Howard and a small group of followers continued to resist until Dacre's horsemen arrived to plug the gap, but by this time Howard had been knocked down three times and was seriously wounded. He was rescued by a detachment of cavalry led by the Bastard Heron, who according to Hall greeted him with the scarcely reassuring remark that 'there was never a nobleman's son so like to be lost as you be on this day'.

Heron and Howard both made their escape, while those of their men who remained on the field sought safety with the Lord Admiral's division on their left. According to Pitscottie, Huntly and Hume then sounded their trumpets and recalled their men to their standards. The chronicler makes this sound easy, but it must have taken some time. The Highland clansmen were accustomed to deciding an encounter with a single charge, and it is unlikely that they had ever practiced rallying and reforming in the middle of a battle. Certainly, we do not hear of this happening in their internal clan wars. Neither were the Borderers noted for their discipline, and they were known to be often reluctant to engage their fellow Borderers serving on the opposite side (see Chapter Nine, below). So although Huntly and Hume were now on the flank of the main English line, opposed only by a few hundred cavalry who could hardly have held them off for long, they were not necessarily in a position to exploit the situation immediately. Pitscottie attributes their inaction to the treachery or cowardice of Hume, who is said to have advised Huntly that by defeating the men opposite them, his Borderers had done all that was expected of them. Huntly disagreed, but his men were still widely scattered; by the time he was ready to move, the opportunity had passed. Alexander Hume survived the battle, but three years later he was arrested and executed for treason. He had fallen out with the regent, the Duke of Albany, but it was also alleged at the time that he was responsible for the death of James. George Buchanan, writing half a century later, went so far as to claim that the king had also survived the fighting, but that Hume had murdered him. This is highly unlikely, but it does indicate the level of suspicion that remained about Hume's conduct on that day.

The Scottish centre then moved to the attack in its turn. King James equipped himself with a pike and took his place in the front rank – a decision which has received its share of criticism from commentators ever since. It was entirely compatible with his character, because he thought it his duty to share the dangers which he expected his subjects to endure, and it was also in the tradition of Scottish warfare that a chief was expected to lead by example. But on the other hand, he was no longer able to issue orders to his army. The duty of the massed pikemen was simply to march against the enemy to their front, and they could be relied on to follow their king as he led them forward, but on both wings of his army were contingents of Highlanders who were left without orders at a time when their intervention might have been valuable. Nevertheless, the schiltrons at first seemed likely to win the battle on their own. The English archers launched the usual storm of arrows as they approached, but the result was very different from what it had been in earlier battles. The *Trewe Encountre* says that the wind and rain put the archers at a disadvantage, but adds that the Scottish front ranks 'wer also as well appointed as was possible at all points with armes and harnesse, Soe that few of thaim were slain with arrows'. Ironically, the Scots had finally found at least a partial answer to the centuries-old problem of English archery, but in doing so they had made their formations more unwieldy than ever. At the bottom of the slope, they crashed into the English line and at first drove it back, but then they ran into the strip of waterlogged ground at the bottom, in which they quickly became bogged down. Unable to maintain their momentum, most of them threw down their unwieldy pikes, so that it seemed to the English 'as if a wood was falling down', and resorted to their swords, but these weapons – though handier in a close-quarters melee – were outreached by the English bills. The heavily armoured Scottish gentlemen who formed the front ranks were still not easy to defeat, but they were floundering in the marsh in their unwieldy armour, and were gradually surrounded and cut to pieces by the more mobile English billmen, who either still kept their footing on the firmer ground on Piper Hill or could easily retreat to it to regroup if they were hard pressed. In a study of the effects of geology on British battles, Younger (2012) concludes that the role of the boggy terrain at Flodden was decisive and that it 'corresponds precisely' to the area where most of the Scottish casualties occurred.

James's own division actually managed to push part of the way up the slope of Piper Hill despite the conditions underfoot, but the earls on their left were quickly brought to a halt, which enabled men from the Lord Admiral's division to take the king's followers in the flank. No quarter was given and the casualties on both sides began to mount. Bishop Ruthal reported that the men in the Scottish front ranks were 'so mighty, large, strong and great men that they would not fall when four or five bills struck on one of them at once' (quoted in Barr, 2001). But the English eventually began to gain the upper hand. The Earl of Bothwell, commanding the Scottish reserve, then made the same error as the Earl of Mar had done at Dupplin Moor (see Chapter Four); he sent his men into the rear of James's division, where they could give no assistance but merely added to the confusion. James kept fighting to the end, and when he eventually fell around 7.00 pm, his death at first went unnoticed amid the carnage. By then, most of the nobility of his kingdom lay dead around him. When his body was identified the next day by Lord Dacre, it was evident that he had died hard. He had an arrow through the jaw, his left hand had been almost hacked off and his throat was cut. No one knows who killed him. A story was later current that Sir Edward Stanley had done the deed, but this was impossible as Stanley was far off on the English left and had yet to play his part in the battle. Edward Hall believed that the story gained currency because later, when Stanley's men were pursuing the fleeing Highlanders, some of them had come across the king's body and, without recognizing it, had picked up some of his possessions.

The more lightly armoured Highlanders would have been better equipped to cope with the boggy ground in the centre, but Huntly's men were still rallying and the other Highland units were over on the right wing, where it seems that they were waiting for orders which never came. They were still in their starting positions when their king was killed, and it was about the same time that Stanley's column – the last detachment of the English army to be committed – began to arrive on their flank, unseen at first in the dead ground below the steep hill slope on the Scots' right. When they realized what was happening, the clansmen turned 90 degrees to their right and charged the enemy, but in this situation the lightness of their armour was a disadvantage. Stanley's archers and billmen caused heavy casualties, and eventually the Highlanders broke and ran; among those left dead on the field were both the earls who had commanded them. Lord Howard reported that the fleeing Scots were pursued for 3 miles, which would have taken them as far as the Tweed. He put the total of Scottish dead at 10,000, and added that 10,000 more would have been killed if the English had been on horseback.

Queen Katherine reported the victory in a letter to King Henry, sending with it a piece of the bloodstained coat that had been stripped from James's body. Katherine's subsequent fate is well known. Though greatly respected by her contemporaries as a diplomat, orator and scholar, a patron of Renaissance philosophy and pioneer of education for women, she failed to give Henry a male heir and he decided to divorce her. She refused to go quietly and the resultant dispute with the Pope drove England out of the Roman Catholic fold, with incalculable consequences to this day. Katherine was forced into retirement and died in 1536 at the age of 50. The Howards were well rewarded for their victory. In 1514, Thomas senior was created 2nd Duke of Norfolk (his father John Howard, who was killed at Bosworth, had been the 1st Duke), while his son, Thomas, became Earl of Surrey. In what was more a deliberate insult to the Scots than a celebration of victory, Norfolk's coat of arms was augmented with a version of the Scottish royal arms showing the lion with an arrow through its throat. More practically, he rose to become Lord Treasurer and Lord High Steward of England before he died in 1524. Thomas junior became the 3rd Duke of Norfolk and followed his father as Lord Treasurer, but in later life fell out of favour with the king, in part because he remained a Roman Catholic and had little sympathy with Henry's reformation of the Church. In December 1546, he was arrested for treason and he was due to be executed on 28 January 1547. However, King Henry happened to die that very morning and Howard was reprieved, although he remained in prison throughout the reign of Henry's Protestant successor, Edward VI, and was only released by Edward's Catholic sister, Mary, when she came to the throne in 1553. He died in the following year.

It is tempting to consider an 'alternative history' scenario in which Henry VIII was in England at the time of James's invasion, and the two monarchs faced each other on the battlefield at Flodden. It is of course pure speculation, but the 22-year-old Henry was a far less experienced commander than the Earl of Surrey, and in his youth he was considered to be just as prone to taking risks as was James. If he was aware that his opposite number was fighting in the front rank, he might well have thought it necessary to do likewise in order to protect the heroic image which he liked to project. If Henry had also been killed, the implications for the succession were far reaching. His wife, Katherine, had already borne several children, but none had lived, which meant that the throne would have passed to his elder sister, Margaret Tudor, the Queen of Scots. It was via the line of descent from Margaret that the English and Scottish thrones were eventually united under the House of Stewart, when Henry's daughter, Elizabeth I, died childless in 1603. It could certainly be argued that both kingdoms would have been saved a great deal of trouble if the union had occurred ninety years earlier.

In reality, the consequences of the defeat for Scotland were disastrous, although the propagandists were soon at work to minimize the political damage, and Bishop Leslie of Ross (Leslie, 1830) almost manages to make it seem like a Scottish victory. The decision to deploy the best armoured men, who were inevitably the wealthiest and most eminent in society, on foot in the front rank may have been tactically sound, but it exposed them to terrible losses in the event of a defeat. In addition to the king, the Scottish dead included the Lord High Treasurer, the Archbishop of St Andrews, the Bishop of the Isles, nine earls, fourteen other lords of parliament, about 300 lesser members of the aristocracy and between 5,000 and 12,000 commoners, depending on which source we believe (Sadler & Serdiville, 2012). This might represent as many as one in every hundred of the people of the country, killed in a single afternoon. In proportion to the population, Scotland's losses on the day of Flodden were at least twenty times as high as those suffered by the

British Army on its worst day in the First World War, 1 July 1916. The quotation at the head of this chapter comes from the song, 'The Flowers of the Forest' by the eighteenth-century writer Jean Elliot, which is sung to the tune of an old lament for the dead of Flodden and still articulates the country's enduring sense of loss.

The battlefield on Branxton and Piper hills was enclosed in the early eighteenth century and is now largely arable fields or pasture, but it has retained much of its original open appearance. It is well served with interpretation boards and a battlefield trail, maintained by the Remembering Flodden project, which enables the most important features to be visited in two or three hours. There is a car park less than a quarter of a mile west of Branxton village (grid reference NT888373), from which a path leads uphill to the memorial on Piper Hill. There is a visitor centre, which together with its opposite number at Carham (see Chapter One) is often claimed to be the smallest in the world, inside an old red telephone box beside the road in Branxton. The village is situated on a minor road leading west from the A697 between Wooler and Coldstream, and is served by occasional buses. Coldstream, where the Scottish army crossed the Tweed, is about 3 miles further north-west on the road to Edinburgh. The castles at Norham, Wark and Etal are ruined, but can be visited in the summer months. The museum at Etal, which is recommended in several older books, appears to have closed permanently. After James left Ford Castle, it remained partially in ruins until the 1540s. It suffered further damage in the Civil War, but was restored in the nineteenth century and is now an outdoor activity centre. It is not normally open to the public, but the impressive exterior can be viewed from the footpath from Ford village to the church. The village is the headquarters of Ford and Etal Estates, who own the battlefield, and has several other sites which are worth visiting. Flodden Edge, where the Scottish army originally intended to fight, is about a mile south of Branxton Hill. It is traversed by several minor roads and footpaths, from which it is possible to admire the views and gain an impression of the strength of the position.

Chapter Nine

The Age of the Reivers

AS IT TURNED out, Flodden was the last great Anglo-Scottish battle to be fought in Northumberland, but it was by no means the end of hostilities. James IV left an heir, James V, who was less than 18 months old at his accession to the throne – yet another in the long list of royal minorities which had plagued Scotland throughout its long confrontation with England. His mother, Queen Margaret, was appointed regent and went on to negotiate a peace with England, but many of the nobility considered her unsuitable for the role, both as a woman and as the sister of their country's arch enemy, Henry VIII. Her reputation suffered still further when in 1514 she married the irresponsible and unpopular Archibald Douglas, the Earl of Angus. Margaret was replaced as regent by John Stewart, 2nd Duke of Albany, who as a son of James II was second in line to the throne, and soon afterwards she fled to England, leaving her husband behind. In 1524, she returned and overthrew Albany, and James – who was still only 12 years old – assumed full royal powers, in theory at least. In truth, he remained the pawn of various contending factions until 1528, when he expelled Archibald Douglas, who had by now been divorced by the queen. During the 1530s, tensions between Scotland and England once again increased, due largely to James's staunch support for the Roman Catholic Church, which persisted despite the efforts of Henry VIII to persuade him to break with it. While Margaret was alive the peace held, but after her death in 1541 Henry, in an obvious act of preparation for war, ordered that those Scots who had settled in Northumberland during the years of peace should be evicted and their crops destroyed to prevent them from returning.

In the following year, he sent an army of 3,000 Borderers under the Warden of the East March, Richard Bowes, to ravage the Scottish side of the frontier. During the sixteenth century, it seems that the fighting along the border was increasingly becoming the responsibility of the Border people themselves, and especially of their lightly equipped and highly mobile horsemen. These were of course the prototypes of the famous Border Reivers, whose blood feuds and small-scale raids have passed into legend (see below, pages 153–156), and the link between warfare and their less-organized activities is clear. On the one hand, the equipment and tactics which they employed in their raids had been developed over the centuries on the battlefield, but on the other, as George MacDonald Fraser (1971) has pointed out, they would no doubt have regarded the episodes of warfare as unwelcome distractions from their main business activities.

The Borderers who attacked Scotland in 1542 were accompanied by Archibald Douglas, who had defected to Henry after his expulsion by the Scots. Their ultimate aim was to burn the town of Kelso, or so James V alleged in a letter to his English counterpart (*State Papers of Henry VIII*, Part IV continued, CCCXCII). However, Bowes and Douglas were surprised at Haddon Rig near Kelso on 24 August by a Scottish detachment led by George Gordon, Earl of Huntly, and Sir Walter Lindsay of Torphichen. Lindsay did not wait for Huntly to bring up the main body, but led his 2,000 Border horse in a charge which routed the English at the first clash. The renegade Earl of Angus was one of the first to flee. In November 1542, a large army of around 15,000 Scots invaded England in retaliation, taking the western route into Cumberland. Their official commander was Robert, Lord Maxwell, the Warden of the West March, but confusion soon grew about who was actually in charge. Two different sixteenth-century accounts allege either that the royal cup bearer, Oliver Sinclair, produced a warrant from the king placing him in command, or that he simply delivered a message from James confirming Maxwell's appointment, which was somehow misunderstood. Whatever the case, many of the Scottish nobles refused to obey Sinclair, whom they regarded – with justification – as a mere courtier with no military experience. After crossing the border, they were led astray by local guides who were either incompetent or treacherous, and when on the 24th they were attacked by 3,000 English Border horse led by Sir Thomas Wharton, they found themselves trapped against the River Esk and the bog known as Solway Moss. The Scots were thrown into complete confusion and received no orders from their feuding leaders, and after putting up a fierce fight in their own defence they were forced to surrender. Maxwell and Sinclair were captured and later ransomed; both their names appear in a long list of Scottish captives – with the value of all their property and incomes and the names of those who would stand surety for them – in the *State Papers* (Part IV continued, CCCCIX). However, the most notable casualty of the debacle was said to have been James V himself, who died only two weeks later. He was only 30 years old, and it is often alleged that his demise was brought on by the humiliation of the defeat, combined with disappointment when his wife, Mary of Guise, gave birth to a girl. He had suffered from poor health for several years, which may have been the reason why he had not led the doomed army in person.

James was succeeded by his newborn daughter, Mary, who was known ever afterwards as Mary, Queen of Scots. The regent, James Hamilton, 2nd Earl of Arran, pursued a peace policy with Henry VIII which led to the Treaty of Greenwich, signed in July 1543. There were in fact two separate treaties: one was yet another pledge to maintain peace between the two countries as long as Henry or Mary should live, while the second provided for the marriage of Mary to Henry's son, Edward, the future King Edward VI. This would have accomplished the union of the two crowns, but on terms which, as most of the Scottish nobility saw it, were overwhelmingly favourable to England. The Archbishop of St Andrews, Cardinal Beaton, led the opposition to the marriage, and feelings ran so high that two pitched battles were fought around Glasgow early in 1544 between Hamilton and his opponents. But by then it was too late for the peace party. In December of the previous year, the Scottish parliament had refused to approve the treaty, and less than a week later Henry's herald had delivered his declaration of war. In May 1544, an English army commanded by the Earl of Hertford landed from the sea and attacked Edinburgh. They were unable to take the castle, but looted and then burned the rest of the town. Henry had instructed Hertford to inflict the same fate on St Andrews, but the earl was reluctant to overextend his forces, and instead marched back to Berwick overland.

Nevertheless, the English attacks on southern Scotland continued, and at the beginning of 1545 Sir Ralph Eure and Sir Brian Laiton crossed the border with an exceptionally large raiding party consisting of 2,200 Borderers – of whom 700 were disaffected Scots – and 3,000 German and Spanish mercenaries, who appear to have been pikemen. After a rampage which was said to have been unusually destructive even by Border standards, the invaders were intercepted on 27 February by a considerably smaller Scottish force while marching along Dere Street, the Roman road which led south-east from Melrose towards Jedburgh. The Scots were led by the earls of Arran and Angus, who had temporarily set aside their differences, but they seemed to have numbered no more than 2,000. The traditional site of the encounter, which became known as the Battle of Ancrum Moor, is on Lilliard's Edge, a long, low ridge which runs from south-west–north-east and forms the watershed between the Tweed and Teviot rivers, but recent analysis has argued that it may have taken place on Trowpenny Ridge, about a mile further south (Parkhouse, 2023). A detachment of Scottish horse made a feint attack on the English before retreating in apparent confusion over the summit of the ridge. The English pursued them, only to find the main Scottish army waiting in a concealed position on the far side of the hill. The Scots charged from close range, aided by the setting sun behind them and the wind which blew smoke from the English arquebuses back towards them. Lindesay of Pitscottie says that the Scots' pikes were longer than those of the 'Inglismen' – by which he presumably means their foreign mercenaries – as a result of which they pushed Eure's men back over the hill and down the other side, knocking many of them to the ground. Upon seeing this, the Scots serving in the English army tore off the red crosses that they had been wearing to identify themselves and turned on their former allies. A nineteenth-century plaque on Lilliard's Edge commemorates the 'fair maiden Lilliard', a Scottish woman who was said to have taken up arms to avenge the death of her lover and inflicted heavy losses on the English, but there is no contemporary evidence for her existence. The English, however, were decisively defeated. Eure, Laiton and 800 of their men were killed, 1,000 more were captured and the rest fled.

The Battle of Pinkie

After the death of Henry VIII in January 1547, England had a taste of the problems of a royal minority which had so often plagued Scotland. Henry's 9-year-old son succeeded to the throne as Edward VI, with his uncle, Edward Seymour, Duke of Somerset, acting as Lord Protector or regent. Within two years, Somerset's unpopular religious reforms and financial mismanagement had led to his downfall, but in the meantime he continued to pursue Henry's war policy in the North, still hoping to force the Scots to agree to Queen Mary's marriage to King Edward. In September 1547, he personally led an army of around 17,000 men across the border in the direction of Edinburgh. Most of these men were the usual northern levies, armed much as they had been at Flodden with bills and bows, but there were also contingents of mercenaries armed with primitive handguns or arquebuses – Germans on foot, and Spaniards and Italians who fought from horseback. The Earl of Arran raised an army to meet him, and the two sides met at the Battle of Pinkie, or Pinkie Cleugh, which was fought on 10 September at Inveresk, near Musselburgh on the East Lothian coast. The result underlined one of the key themes of our story: Scottish armies continued to rely heavily on one tactic: the schiltrons of close-order spearmen. These had ostensibly been upgraded to incorporate the innovations which had been made on the continent since the 1470s, and gunpowder artillery was being used in increasing numbers to support them, but in essence they were still the formations that had fought under Wallace at Stirling Bridge, Bruce at Bannockburn and James IV at Flodden. Where they could seize the initiative, as they had at Bannockburn and Ancrum Moor, or where the enemy could be induced to throw himself in disorder on steady spearmen, as had happened at Stanhope Park, the schiltrons could be unstoppable. But in a pitched battle where the English armies had time to deploy to take advantage of the ground, the inflexibility and predictability of the Scottish attacks made them all too easy to counter.

Arran's plan was apparently to repeat the tactics that had given him victory at Ancrum Moor, and on the day before the battle he attempted an ambush at Fawside Brae, where he hid his infantry behind a hill and sent out 1,500 Scottish Border horse to try and lure their English counterparts into a rash pursuit. Unfortunately for the Scots, the English cavalry commander, Lord Grey of Wilton, timed his charge so well that he caught the Borderers just as they turned away and routed them. In view of his previous success, Arran can hardly be accused of not understanding the capabilities of his spearmen, but when the main battle was joined on the following day he may have felt that he had no choice but to send them forward in a mass charge of the sort that had failed at Flodden. The English now had cavalry superiority as well as greater strength in artillery, augmented by the guns of their fleet anchored in the Firth of Forth. So rather than stand on the defensive waiting to be shot down, Arran ordered a charge while Somerset was still manoeuvring into position. The Scottish pikes made rapid progress at first and repulsed a charge by the heavily armoured English men-at-arms, but this forced them to halt temporarily and gave Somerset's guns time to deploy and open fire at close range. The Highlanders in Arran's army, whose archers provided much of his missile power, were unfamiliar with the effects of artillery and soon fell back, leaving the schiltrons exposed to a lethal fire from the English bowmen and the arquebusiers, as well as the heavy guns. According to William Patten, the Earl of Arran himself was the next to run away, followed by most of his army. But despite the defeat and the damage that the English armies continued to inflict on the Border counties, the Scots continued to resist, and in August 1548 Mary was smuggled to safety in France, where she was destined to marry the young Dauphin, the future Francis II. She later returned to Scotland but was deposed in 1567, fled to England and remained there until 1587, when her cousin, Queen Elizabeth, had her executed as a potential rival for the English throne through her descent from Henry VII. Her son, James VI, succeeded as King of Scots.

The Origins of the Reivers

The sixteenth century is best known in Border history for the exploits of the 'reivers'. These freelance raiders came from families on both sides of the frontier and were often recruited into the Border horse units in English and Scottish armies, but just as often fought and raided each other unofficially, sometimes with the tacit support of the government on their side of the frontier, on other occasions in defiance of all authority. The word 'reiver' was derived from an Old English verb, 'reifian', which meant to rob (Groom, 2022). Most of what we know of their exploits dates from the century after the Battle of Flodden, but their origins were much more remote in time. In the tenth and eleventh centuries, when the Anglo-Scottish border was coming into being along the line of the River Tweed, many of the upland areas were still very sparsely inhabited. Much of the region west of the Tweed Valley was never suitable for dense human settlement because of high altitude and poor soils, but even in the early Middle Ages, people were gradually encroaching into the hills from both north and south as the population increased, and by the fourteenth century their settlements were coming into more frequent contact with each other, a process which eventually gave rise to a more coherent cross-border society (Barrow, 1992). However, in Professor Barrow's view, the Anglo-Scottish border, even in the twelfth century, was a political compromise which did not necessarily reflect the demographics of settlement (Bartlett & Mackay, 1990). At the eastern end of the border, the Tweed must have formed an easily recognizable line of demarcation, but we should nevertheless not assume that after the Battle of Carham everyone living on the south bank saw themselves as English, while those on the north bank automatically identified as Scots. It seems that although the Gaelic language was in the ascendent in most of Scotland at this time (Barrow, 1992; Woolf, 2007), it never made serious inroads into Lothian. So a similar Northumbrian dialect of English was still spoken on both sides of the border, just as it had been in the tenth century when Northumbrian political power had extended as far north as Edinburgh.

By the sixteenth century, the families on opposite sides had intermarried extensively and continued to do so, a process made easier by their shared language and culture. This emerging 'border society' was both a consequence of the Anglo-Scottish Wars and one of the causes of their continuation. A list of feudal tenants in Cumberland, drawn up in 1212 and incorporated into the *Liber Feodorum* (*Book of Fees*) around 1300, concludes with the statement that if the king's army went into Scotland, those listed were to provide an advance guard when entering the country and a rearguard when returning (Crump, ed., 1920). This suggests that English rulers were well aware of the value of local knowledge in scouting for an army and screening it against the enemy. There is no indication in the document that the tenants of Cumberland were equipped in any way differently from the rest of the army, but it is tempting to see in them the distant origins of the lightly armoured and highly mobile Border Horse of the sixteenth century. Certainly by the 1290s, the predecessors of these men – carrying lances and swords but wearing only quilted armour and helmets, mounted on small, agile horses – were beginning to appear in the borderlands. These were the 'hobilars', so called after their little ponies, or 'hobbies', who were first recruited in Ireland by Edward I but by 1300 were being supplemented by native Englishmen, riding slightly larger horses but otherwise similarly equipped (Heath, 1982). They were particularly valuable as scouts, but their mobility also came in useful for raiding the enemy's villages and driving off his cattle, an activity which was a normal part of regular medieval warfare, but which of course also lent itself to private enterprise. The sort of freelance blackmail and kidnapping activities which we associate with the reivers of the sixteenth century were already common as early as the fourteenth, to judge from a document quoted by Philip Deakin ('The Church of St Peter, Chillingham', in Bahn & Mutimer, 2016). A particular date in January 1395 was remembered because, among other events, 'John Horsley had the misfortune to be carried off by the Scots, but his capture was evenly balanced by John Wytton, who laid hands on Thomas Turnbull, a Scot, and lodged him in Chillingham castle. That same day Robert Horne was seized by Sir Thomas Grey of Heton and carried to Norham Castle against his will.' Low-level violence was normal, and even ostensibly friendly contacts between Englishmen and Scotsmen could come to resemble all-out warfare. Fraser (1971) cites the example of a football match between two teams of villagers from opposite sides of the border, which ended with two men dead, thirty carried off as prisoners and many others injured, especially John Whytfeild, whose 'bowells came out, but are sowed up againe'. Conversely, actual war could sometimes take on the aspect of a game, because the Borderers generally attached a higher priority to local relationships than to the ambitions of their respective monarchs, and were reluctant to risk starting a deadly feud by engaging their opposite numbers too enthusiastically. William Patten tells how at the Battle of Pinkie, the English and Scottish border horsemen were seen conversing peaceably, only resorting to their weapons and pretending to fence with each other when they realized that they were being observed, reminding him of 'the running at base in an uplandish town, where the match is made for a quart of good ale' (Cooper, 2008).

The system of border marches which regulated affairs along the frontier is thought to have originated in the statutes drawn up by a meeting of twelve knights from each country which was presided over by the Sheriffs of Northumberland, Berwick and Roxburgh in 1249, during the reigns of Henry III of England and Alexander III of Scotland (Pease, 1912). The territories on each side of the border were divided into East, Middle and West Marches, each of which was under the control of a Warden, reporting to the Lord Warden who oversaw the entire border. The Wardens were appointed by the Crown, and well-known local names like Percy in England and Douglas in Scotland were prominent among them. It was the responsibility of these men to enforce the March Law relating to the Borders, to deter incursions from across the frontier, and if required to undertake military campaigns in support of their respective governments. The northern part of Northumbria fell within the English East March, which for most of the period between the fourteenth and sixteenth centuries was administered from Berwick-upon-Tweed, and guarded the border along the Tweed as far west as Carham. The boundary between the East and Middle Marches ran from east to west a few miles south of Wooler. The main administrative centre for the Middle March was Alnwick, and its border with its Scottish equivalent included the wild country around the Cheviot and Upper Redesdale.

Border Weapons and Equipment

The sixteenth-century Borderer was less heavily armoured than contemporary men-at-arms; he was unlikely to have been able to afford full plate armour, even if his little 'hobby' had been capable of carrying the weight. Coats of mail, however, were still in use, and the earlier 'aketon', or padded cotton body armour, had been largely replaced by the jack, a leather or linen garment which looked superficially similar but was strengthened by the addition of iron or horn plates riveted beneath the outer covering. Helmets, the famous 'steel bonnets', tended to follow European fashions, so as the century progressed simple kettle hats or pot helmets were replaced by visored burgonets, or by morions with curved brims and combs or crests on the top. The traditional lance and sword remained in use, supplemented for men on foot by English bills or their Scottish equivalent, the Jedburgh Stave, which John Major describes simply as 'a piece of iron four feet long [fastened] to the end of a stout staff' (Cannan, 2009). Nevertheless, not all Borderers were so well armed. A muster of 1584, cited by Pease (1912), listed for the East March 827 infantry with both jack and spear, and 1,347 with spear only. The equivalent figures for mounted men were 267 and 546. Thus, fewer than one-in-ten of the able-bodied men were equipped as the 'classic' Border horse with both armour and lance. Missile weapons were usually bows, which were especially popular with the English Borderers, or small crossbows, suitable for use on foot or mounted, which were known as latches. Arquebuses and pistols were in use by the end of the century, but they were expensive and difficult to maintain, and even at that late date they seem to have been uncommon. Fraser quotes a muster roll from Leith Ward, Cumberland, in 1580, which showed more than 800 archers but only nine arquebusiers, while another muster of 2,500 men from 1583 mentions no firearms among them at all.

It was not only men and horses that fought in the Border Wars. The sixteenth-century writer, Hector Boece, describes three breeds of dog 'of marvellous nature' which were unique to Scotland (Ritchie, 1920). One was the 'sleuthound', or 'sleuth hound', a sort of bloodhound which was used by the Borderers to track down thieves and stolen stock by scent, and was so skilled at this job that it would not lose the trail even if a fugitive tried to shake it off by wading through running water. The sleuth hound was red or black in colour, with small spots on its body. It was no bigger than a rache, which was a type of hound used for hunting and probably similar in size to a modern foxhound, but, says Boece, it would not only track a thief, but when it caught him would 'invade him with great crueltie'. He adds that according to the laws of the Borders, anyone who refused a sleuth hound entry to his property when it was on the trail of a criminal was considered to be an accomplice in his crime. Despite Boece's contention that such dogs were found nowhere else but in Scotland, 'slewdogges' performing a similar role, although perhaps different in appearance, did exist on the English side of the border. Fraser suggests that they resembled the modern Cumberland trail hound, which is basically a lean, fast foxhound. The same author says that these dogs were highly valued and could be worth as much as ten pounds each, so that, not surprisingly, they were themselves often stolen. In England, a levy to pay for their maintenance was collected by local officials, and as late as 1616 those refusing to pay could be imprisoned until they did so (Pease, 1912).

The 'Battle' of the Redeswire

What is sometimes described as the last battle ever fought between the independent kingdoms of England and Scotland took place as late as 1575 at the spot known as the Redeswire, at the head of Redesdale. In reality this was more of a minor affray among Borders families that broke out during one of the regular Truce Days at which officials from both sides met on the border to discuss matters of mutual concern. The Scottish Keeper of Liddesdale, Sir John Carmichael, demanded that an Englishman named Farnstein, who had been accused of theft, be handed over to him, but his English counterpart, the Warden Sir John Forster, replied that the offender had escaped and was no longer in his custody. Forster, a hard-bitten veteran of the battles of Solway Moss and Pinkie, was well known to be in league with a number of habitual criminals, so Carmichael and many of his followers doubted his word and insulted the Englishmen present, whereupon a fight broke out. The outnumbered Scots were forced into a retreat, but on their way home they met up with a group of their countrymen from Jedburgh, who were coming late to the meeting. Thus reinforced, they returned and defeated the English, of whom twenty-five were killed, including the Keeper of Redesdale, Sir George Heron, and his brother. Forster and several others were taken prisoner. Carmichael handed over the prisoners to the Earl of Morton, who was then acting as regent for the 11-year-old King James VI, but not wishing to provoke the English any further, Morton ordered them released with an apology. Queen Elizabeth in London was furious, but the Scottish government was so determined to avoid a war that it handed over Carmichael for trial. However, a court at York accepted that Forster's men had started the fight, and Carmichael was released to resume a distinguished career in the service of King James. He served as an ambassador to England in the 1590s, and was on the verge of retirement when he was murdered by members of the notorious Armstrong clan in an ambush in 1600. Forster also continued in office, and ten years later was present at a further affray when his son-in-law, Lord Russell, was shot dead at another Truce Day on top of the hill known as Windy Gyle. The English blamed the Scottish Warden, Sir Thomas Kerr of Ferniehurst, for allowing the shooting to happen, and another fight was only narrowly averted. James VI removed Ferniehurst from his post, but he died soon afterwards and so was never brought to trial. Therefore, the murder was never officially solved. Forster, however, lived into his 80s and managed to die in his bed, at Bamburgh, in 1602. With this anti-climax, the long history of the Anglo-Scottish Border Wars in Northumberland came to an end.

Sites associated with the Reivers are to be found all over Northumberland, as well as on the Scottish side of the border. The OS historical map *In Search of the Border Reivers* (Ordnance Survey, 1998), although now out of print, remains an excellent guide to several hundred such locations. The Redeswire, where the 'battle' of 1575 took place, is now known as Carter Bar (grid reference NT698068), and is located at the point where the A68 from Otterburn to Jedburgh crosses the watershed on the border between England and Scotland. Near the road is a monument with the inscription, 'On this ridge July 7th 1575 was fought one of the last border frays known as the Raid of the Redeswire'. The summit of Windy Gyle is also on the watershed which constitutes the border, about 4 miles south-west of the Cheviot, at grid reference NT855152. The crumbling pile of stones on top of the hill known as Lord Russell's Cairn is not connected with the incident of 1585, but is in fact a Bronze Age burial mound. In good weather, both sites provide spectacular views across the border country.

Conclusion

THE LONG AND entangled history of the English and Scottish royal families reached its inevitable conclusion in 1603, when Elizabeth I of England died childless. The next in line to the throne was her cousin, James VI of Scotland, and it had long been accepted by the political establishment in both countries that he would eventually unite the kingdoms. He had in fact been receiving a subsidy from Elizabeth for the last seventeen years, and thanks to some protracted behind-the-scenes manoeuvring by agents of both countries he was able to succeed her without any significant unrest. The violent hostility that English or English-backed claimants to the Scottish throne had always encountered in Scotland was not reciprocated south of the border, perhaps because England was far richer and more populous, and so had less reason to fear being absorbed by its neighbour. James clearly believed that the union was not merely personal, but was the fulfilment of God's plan for the whole island to be one and 'indivisible' under a single divinely appointed ruler. To reflect this, he insisted on being described as 'King of Great Britain', even though the English parliament at least refused to accept this as a legal title. With the union of the two crowns under the Stewart (to the English the Stuart) dynasty, the border lost its military significance overnight, the Marches on both sides were abolished and James decreed that the counties on either side should henceforth be known as the 'Middle Shires'. The independent and turbulent Borderers could not be so easily wished out of existence, but to a man of James's views, the presence of a lawless frontier in the middle of a united kingdom was of course intolerable, and he resolved to remove it by the most drastic measures. Already in the Highlands and Islands of Scotland he had attempted to subdue any hint of separatism by measures which amounted almost to genocide. In 1598, he had authorized a private company of Lowlanders known as the Gentlemen Adventurers of Fife to colonize the 'barbarous' Isle of Lewis, which was then part of the ancestral territory of the MacLeod clan, dealing with the inhabitants by 'extirpation' if necessary. This enterprise had failed thanks to the resistance put up by the MacLeods, but in 1609 James introduced the Statutes of Iona, one clause of which is often interpreted as an attempt to eradicate the Gaelic culture and language by forcing their nobility to have their eldest sons educated in English. Beginning in the same year, the king also promoted the Plantation of Ulster, completing the destruction of traditional Irish society in large parts of the north of the island by settling Protestant Scottish and English immigrants on lands confiscated from Catholics. The Borderers fared no better. Despite their reputation as an independent society owing allegiance to neither Edinburgh nor London, it quickly became apparent that it was only the tension along the border that had sustained them for so long. As soon as their light horsemen were no longer required for military service against their neighbours, the authorities on both sides could concentrate on disarming them. And without the option to shake off pursuit by the forces of one kingdom by crossing into the other, they soon found that they had nowhere to hide.

The new government of Great Britain could now apply overwhelming force to the task of rooting out the reivers, beginning with a proclamation by James's Border Commissioners in 1605, which ordered the disarmament of men living in Redesdale and other specified localities (Pease, 1912). These operations were more a matter of law enforcement than military campaigns, and there was no significant resistance beyond a few ambushes of royal officials by raiding gangs, but it still took nearly twenty years to complete the job. As George MacDonald Fraser has recorded, it was often carried out with the sort of brutality and vindictiveness which characterized King James's attitude to the more remote parts of his kingdom. Fraser gives several examples of officials being permitted to carry out executions without trial, on the pretext that the urgency of the situation and the risk of prisoners escaping precluded the normal processes of law. This naturally led to the temptation to settle old scores, especially since many of the king's men were themselves from Border families. Other local magnates managed to enrich themselves at the expense of their neighbours. Fraser points out that the Grahams of Eskdale in Cumbria, who were persecuted with particular zeal, allegedly for their record as reivers, had also committed the offence of occupying a fertile country which the Duke of Cumberland coveted for himself. Most of the Grahams, like many of their contemporaries, were eventually hanged, imprisoned or forced to emigrate, principally to Ireland, where they became reluctant agents of the Protestant settlement. As also happened in the case of the Highlanders, any warlike elements among the surviving Borderers were neutralized by recruiting them for service on James's foreign expeditions. For despite his reputation as a lover of peace, the king was unable to remain entirely aloof from the troubles on the continent, and his campaign against what he regarded as dangerous separatism in Ireland and the north of Scotland continued unabated. In 1604, he had succeeded in making a lasting peace with Spain, Elizabeth I's old enemy. But fifteen years later, when the old religious antagonisms in Europe were reignited in the Thirty Years' War, he was forced to send an army to Germany to support his son-in-law, the Elector Frederick V of the Palatinate, in his claim to the throne of Bohemia. The presence of the Border horsemen was just as useful in these theatres as their absence was welcome at home. To take just two examples, in the year of James's accession, 2,000 Scots from Liddesdale served in the Low Countries against the Spanish, and 100 Englishmen from Redesdale and Tynedale were sent to fight in Ireland in 1607. James is said to have commented of the Liddesdale men that he was 'not altogether displeased that this rabble should be taken out of the kingdom', and even hinted to the Spanish ambassador, who complained about their activities, that his master was welcome to recruit more of them himself (Fraser, 1971).

Despite all of James's efforts, the evolution of a genuinely united kingdom was a protracted and often violent process. In 1638, the attempts of his son, Charles I, to impose a common ecclesiastical doctrine and organization on England and Scotland provoked strong resistance in presbyterian Scotland and led to the National Covenant, whose signatories pledged to resist the imposition of Anglican bishops. In the following year, the First Bishops' War saw the king attempt unsuccessfully to suppress the Covenanters, as his opponents were called. The only major engagement of this war was at the Brig of Dee in Aberdeenshire, where Covenanters led by James Graham, 5th Marquis of Montrose, defeated a Royalist army. But an English army was assembled near Berwick, and Charles threatened to destroy any Scottish force which approached within 10 miles of the border. This would have been difficult to achieve as the English were mainly local militia, while the Scots were stronger in numbers and led by a talented soldier, Alexander Leslie, 1st Earl of Leven. Leslie had served as a field marshal in the Swedish Army, which was generally recognized as the best in Europe. On this occasion a truce was arranged, and no fighting took place on the border. But inevitably the truce soon broke down, and in August of the following year, Leven and Montrose invaded Northumberland. They bypassed Berwick, which was strongly garrisoned, but the outnumbered English forces withdrew to Durham, leaving the Scots to take possession of Newcastle with hardly a fight. The only engagement of the campaign was a skirmish at Newburn, 6 miles west of the town, in which a small English force under Viscount Conway tried to prevent Leven from fording the river. The opposing artillery was deployed on opposite banks and commenced a long-range duel which the Scots won, allowing their infantry to cross. A monument and interpretation panel commemorating the 'Battle of Newburn Ford' can be found just south of the river off Newburn Bridge Road, Newburn (grid reference NZ163650). The area is easily accessible with good footpaths, and the Battlefields Trust website describes the site as 'particularly rewarding', despite the small scale of the battle.

By this time, Newcastle was of strategic importance as the source of most of London's coal, but Charles was in no position to retake it because of the ongoing standoff between him and the English parliament, which kept him perpetually short of money. In September, he called what was to become known as the Long Parliament, which refused either to cooperate with the king or to allow itself to be dissolved, and eventually outlasted Charles himself. The king therefore had no choice but to negotiate another truce, which not only left the Scots in control of Northumberland and County Durham but paid them £850 a day towards the costs of the occupation, a redrawing of the border which had no precedent since the days of King Stephen, 500 years earlier. In August 1641, the Treaty of London brought an end to the Bishops' Wars and the Scots peacefully evacuated Northumberland, but in the following year a full-scale civil war broke out in England between the king and parliament. Charles appointed William Cavendish, the Earl of Newcastle, as governor of that town, and he quickly restored order in Northumberland. In June 1643, he defeated the Parliamentarians at Adwalton Moor in Yorkshire, bringing most of northern England under royalist control and earning for himself the title of Marquis. However, a desperate Parliament then turned to the Scots for assistance, and in September it approved a new agreement named the Solemn League and Covenant, in effect signing up to the Scottish Covenanters' campaign against the king and his plans for the Church. Early in the following year a Scottish army, led once again by the Earl of Leven, marched into Northumberland. It besieged Newcastle and marched on into County Durham to link up with the English Parliamentarian army, and on 2 July 1664, at Marston Moor near York, their combined forces crushed the Royalist army led by the Marquis of Newcastle and Prince Rupert. The Earl of Newcastle's own regiment of foot, known as the 'Whitecoats', which had been raised mainly from his tenants in Northumberland, refused to surrender and was almost wiped out. When Newcastle finally fell to Leven's army in October, the war in the county was over, but the Scots remained in occupation.

In April 1646, King Charles surrendered to the Scottish army which was besieging Newark, and they took him north to Newcastle, where he was held prisoner until the beginning of 1647. In exchange for a substantial payment, the Scots agreed to evacuate Northumberland and hand over the king, who was executed by his Parliamentarian enemies two years later. In February 1647, the Scottish troops left for the last time. Cavendish had fled to the continent, but returned after the restoration of the monarchy by Charles's son, Charles II, in 1660 and reclaimed his estates. Five years later, in recognition of his services to the royalist cause, he was awarded the title of 1st Duke of Newcastle.

Many of the people of Northumberland remained loyal to the Stuart dynasty through the turbulent years that followed the restoration. Charles II's brother succeeded him in 1685 as King James II of England and VII of Scotland, but his conversion to Roman Catholicism led to the Glorious Revolution of 1688, in which he was forced into exile and replaced on the throne by the Dutch Protestant prince, William of Orange. Several attempts were made by the pro-Stuart party, known as the Jacobites, to restore him or his successors. After James's death in 1701, his claim to the throne passed to his son, James Francis Edward Stuart, who was known by his supporters as King James VIII and by his opponents as the 'Old Pretender'. In two attempts by the Jacobites to seize power, in 1715 and 1745, the people of Northumberland once again took up arms. Richard Lomas (1996) estimates that in the 1715 rebellion, at least seventy-seven of the Northumberland gentry joined the rebels, accompanied by a couple of hundred of their followers. They joined up with a Jacobite force from the Scottish Borders to invade Lancashire, but were defeated at Preston in November. Ten of the ringleaders died in battle or in prison or were executed, but no fighting took place in Northumberland itself.

Although the route into England through the county had been the one favoured by invaders from Scotland since time immemorial, on the most recent occasion that an army crossed the frontier, during the last

Jacobite rebellion in 1745, it was reduced to the status of a diversion. However, this was due more to the particular conditions prevailing at the time than to any permanent change in the strategic significance of the eastern route. In September 1745, the Jacobites led by Prince Charles Edward Stuart – 'The Young Pretender', or 'Bonnie Prince Charlie' – occupied Edinburgh and effectively took control of Scotland. They then began to make plans for an invasion of England with the aim of placing Charles's father, James, whom the Jacobites still considered to be the legitimate heir of the Stuart kings, on the throne of Great Britain. On 21 September, the prince's forces defeated a government army at Prestonpans in East Lothian, and Charles was eager to exploit the moral advantage which the victory gave him to cross into England and engage the main government force under General George Wade, which was mustering near Newcastle. Wade was an experienced commander, but at 72 years old he was no longer as energetic as he had been, and his men were poorly equipped and supplied, many of them lacking even shoes. Nevertheless, many of Charles's advisors considered the whole invasion strategy too risky, preferring to consolidate their control in Scotland and wait for help from their French allies. This, however, was unrealistic because of the impossibility of raising any more money or recruits from Scotland, and the restless nature of the prince's Highland troops, who would simply have gone home if they had been expected to wait on the defensive indefinitely. Lord George Murray thus proposed an advance into Lancashire via Carlisle, combined with a feint into Northumberland, which was eventually adopted as a compromise. In its favour, Murray cited the vulnerability of the obsolete fortifications at Carlisle as opposed to those at Berwick, the shorter distance from the western end of the border to London and the greater likelihood of receiving reinforcements in strongly Jacobite Lancashire (Duffy, 2015). However, it seems likely that a stronger motive was the desire to avoid staking the fate of the whole rebellion on a pitched battle against Wade.

In the event, the Jacobites outmanoeuvred the government armies and advanced as far south as Derby, but they failed to press their advantage, withdrew from England without fighting a major battle and were finally defeated back in Scotland, at the Battle of Culloden, in April 1746. The continuing strategic importance of Northumberland was underlined by the fact that by ignoring it, the Jacobites had left Edinburgh exposed, and within a few weeks government forces had reoccupied it. Understandably, it has been a matter of speculation ever since whether Charles Edward might have been wiser to seek an immediate confrontation with Wade, in which event Northumberland would once again have been the scene of a battle that left its mark in history. As it happened, the Jacobite diversionary force, which consisted of cavalry under the command of Colonel Henry Kerr, crossed the border east of the Cheviot and advanced on Wooler, but the government cavalrymen who were based there fled before a shot could be fired. Local Jacobites devised a plan to seize Newcastle and hold it for Prince Charlie when his army approached, but they never had a chance to put it into action. Most of the people of the town remained loyal to the reigning king, George II, even when the neighbouring countryside prepared to welcome the prince, thus allegedly earning their nickname of 'Geordies'. Wade managed to march his men 20 miles to Hexham, where he learnt that the enemy had already slipped past him on the other side of the Pennines, and then back again. They had seen no action, but this one march in bad weather and without a proper supply train was enough to virtually destroy them as a fighting force. On this almost farcical note, the last military operations in Northumberland came to an end.

Sources and Recommended Reading

Armstrong, P. & Walsh, S., *Otterburn 1388*, Osprey Campaign Series 164 (Oxford, 2006).

Ascham, R., *Toxophilus* (London, 1545; available online at archerylibrary.com).

Bahn, P. & Mutimer, V. (eds), *Chillingham: Its Cattle, Castle and Church* (Stroud, 2016).

Barr, N., *Flodden* (Stroud, 2001).

Barrow, G.W.S., *Scotland and its Neighbours in the Middle Ages* (London, 1992).

Bartlett, R. & Mackay, A. (eds), *Medieval Frontier Societies* (Oxford, 1990).

Berwick-upon Tweed's 'War with Russia', Friends of Berwick and District Museum and Archives, berwickfriends.org.uk/history.

Bradbury, J., *The Medieval Archer* (Woodbridge, Suffolk, 1985).

Bradbury, J., *The Medieval Siege* (Woodbridge, Suffolk, 1992).

Breverton, T., *Owain Glyndwr* (Stroud, 2013).

Brie, F., *The Brut, or the Chronicles of England* (London, 1906).

Brown, M., *The Wars of Scotland, 1214–1371* (Edinburgh, 2004).

Burne, A.H., *More Battlefields of England* (London, 1952).

Cannan, F., *Scottish Arms and Armour* (Shire Publications, Oxford, 2009).

Chibnall, M. (trans.), *The Ecclesiastical History of Orderic Vitalis* (Oxford, 1990).

Child, F.W., *The English and Scottish Popular Ballads*, Part IV, Chapter 161, 'The Battle of Otterburn' (London & Cambridge, Massachusetts, 1889).

Childs, W. & Taylor, J. (eds), *The Anonimalle Chronicle 1307 to 1334* (Cambridge, 1991).

Cooper, J. & Turner, G., *Scottish Renaissance Armies 1513–1550*, Osprey Elite 167 (Oxford, 2008).

Creighton, O. & Higham, R., *Medieval Town Walls: An Archaeology and Social History of Urban Defence* (Stroud, 2005).

Crump, C. (ed.), *Liber Feodorum, The Book of Fees, Commonly Called Testa de Nevill*, Part I, AD 1198–1242 (HMSO, London, 1920; also available via The Internet Archive at archive.org; in Latin).

Cunningham, S., *Katherine of Aragon and an Army for the North in 1513* (blog.nationalarchives.org.uk, 20 May 2020).

Dalton, P., *Conquest, Anarchy and Lordship: Yorkshire 1066–1154* (Cambridge, 2002).

Davies, R., *The Revolt of Owain Glyn Dwr* (Oxford, 1995).

Duffy, C., *Fight for a Throne: The Jacobite '45 Reconsidered* (Solihull, 2015).

Durham, K., *Border Reiver 1513–1603*, Osprey Warrior Series 154 (Oxford, 2011).

Durham, K., *Strongholds of the Border Reivers*, Osprey Fortress Series 70 (Oxford, 2008).

Edmonds, F., 'Carham: The Western Perspective', in McGuigan & Woolf (eds) (Edinburgh, 2018).

Embleton, G., *Medieval Military Costume Recreated in Colour Photographs*, Europa military Special no. 8 (The Crowood Press, Marlborough, 2000).

Foard, G. & Morris, R., *The Archaeology of English Battlefields*, Council for British Archaeology Research Report 168 (York, 2012).

Foster, S., *Picts, Gaels and Scots* (Edinburgh, 2014).

Fraser, G.M., *The Steel Bonnets: Story of the Anglo-Scottish Border Reivers* (London, 1971).

Goodman, A. & Took, A., *War and Border Societies in the Middle Ages* (London, 1992).

Goodwin, G., *Fatal Rivalry: Flodden 1513* (London, 2013).

Grant, A., *Independence and Nationhood: Scotland 1306–1469* (Edinburgh, 1984).

Grant, A., 'The Otterburn War From a Scottish Point of View', in Goodman & Took (eds) (1992).

Gravett, C., *Norman Knight, AD 950–1204*, Osprey Warrior Series 1 (Oxford, 1993).

Gravett, C., *Norman Stone Castles (1): The British Isles, 1066–1216*, Osprey Fortress Series 13 (Oxford, 2003).

Greenway, D. (trans.), *Henry of Huntingdon: The History of the English People 1000–1154* (Oxford, 1996).

Groom, B., *Northerners: A History* (Manchester, 2022).

Hallam-Baker, C., *The Battle of Flodden: Why and How*, The Remembering Flodden Project (Branxton, Northumberland, 2012).

Hardy, R., *Longbow: A Social and Military History* (Yeovil, 1992).

Hardy, R., 'The Battle of Homildon Hill', in *Battlefield: The Magazine of the Battlefields Trust*, Volume 22, Issue 2 (2017).

Harting, J., *British Animals Extinct Within Historic Times, With Some Account of British Wild White Cattle* (London, 1880).

Heath, I., *Armies and Enemies of the Crusades 1096–1291* (Worthing, 1978).

Heath, I., *Armies of the Dark Ages 600–1066* (Worthing, 1980).

Heath, I., *Armies of the Middle Ages*, Volume I (Worthing, 1982).

Heath, I., *Armies of Feudal Europe 1066–1300* (Worthing, 1989).

Hill, J. & Freiberg, J., *The Medieval Fighting Man: Costume and Equipment 800–1500* (Crowood Press, Marlborough, 2015).

HM Record Commission, *State Papers King Henry the Eighth*, Volume 5, Part IV continued: Correspondence Relative to Scotland and the Borders, 1534–1546 (London, 1836).

Jolliffe, J. (ed. & trans.), *Froissart's Chronicles* (London, 1967).

King, A., 'Fortresses and Fashion Statements: Gentry Castles in Fourteenth Century Northumberland', *Journal of Medieval History*, Volume 33, Number 4 (2007).

King, A. (ed.), *Sir Thomas Gray: Scalacronica 1272–1363* (Woodbridge, 2005).

Laing, D. (ed.), 'A Contemporary Account of the Battle of Flodden', *Proceedings of the Society of Antiquaries of Scotland*, Volume 7 (Edinburgh, 1867).

Leslie, J., Bishop of Ross, *The History of Scotland, From the Death of James I*, Thomson, T. (ed.) (Edinburgh, 1830).

Lindesay of Pitscottie, R., *The History and Chronicles of Scotland* (Edinburgh, 1814).

Livingston, M., *Never Greater Slaughter: Brunanburgh and the Birth of England* (Osprey Publishing, 2021).

Loades, M., *War Bows* (Oxford, 2019).

Lomas, R., *County of Conflict: Northumberland from Conquest to Civil War* (East Linton, 1996).

Lynch, M., *Scotland, A New History* (London, 1992).

Macivor, I., *The Fortifications of Berwick upon Tweed* (HMSO, London, 1972; revised edition 1983).

Matthews, R., *Battlefield Walks Northumberland* (London, 2008).

Maxwell, H. (trans.), *The Chronicle of Lanercost* (Glasgow, 1913).

McGuigan, N. & Woolf, A. (eds), *The Battle of Carham A Thousand Years On* (Edinburgh, 2018).

Michel, F. (trans.), *Chronicle of the War Between the English and the Scots in 1173 & 1174 by Jordan Fantosme* (London, 1840).

Myers, A.R. (ed.), *English Historical Documents 1327–1485* (London, 1969).

Nicolle, D., *Medieval Siege Weapons (1): Western Europe AD 585–1385*, Osprey New Vanguard Series 58 (Oxford, 2002).

Oram, R., *David I; The King Who Made Scotland* (Stroud, 2008).

Ordnance Survey, *In Search of the Border Reivers* (annotated map) (Southampton, 1998).

Oskarsdottir, S. (ed.), *Egil's Saga* (Penguin Classics, London, 2004).

Parkhouse, G., 'The Battle of Ancrum Moor: A New Narrative, *Battlefield, The Magazine of the Battlefields Trust*, Vol. 27, Issue 4 (Summer 2023).

Pease, H., *The Lord Wardens of the Marches of England and Scotland* (London, 1912).

Peers, C., *Offa and the Mercian Wars* (Barnsley, 2012).

Peers, C., *The Highland Battles: Warfare on Scotland's Northern Frontier in the Early Middle Ages* (Barnsley, 2020).

Peers, C., *Clan Battles: Warfare in the Scottish Highlands in the Late Middle Ages* (Barnsley, 2023).

Peter, D., *Journal of the Movements of King Edward I in Scotland, 1296* (De Re Militari, 23 April 2014).

Pollington, S., *The English Warrior From Earliest Times Till 1066* (Hockwold-cum-Wilton, Norfolk, 2006).

Predonanzi, M. & Alberici, V., *The Italian Wars*, Volume 2 (Warwick, 2021).

Rackham, O., *The History of the Countryside* (London, 1986).

Reese, P., *Flodden: A Scottish Tragedy* (Edinburgh, 2003).

Reid, S, *Castles and Tower Houses of the Scottish clans, 1460–1650*, Osprey Fortress Series 46, Oxford, 2006.

Ritchie, J., *The Influence of Man on Animal Life in Scotland* (Cambridge, 1920).

Robson, J., *Border Battles and Battlefields* (Kelso, 1897).

Rogers, C., *War, Cruel and Sharp: English Strategy under Edward III, 1327–1360* (Woodbridge, 2000).

Rose, A., *Kings in the North: The House of Percy in British History* (London, 2002).

Rothwell, H., *The Chronicle of Walter of Guisborough* (The Royal Historical Society, London, 1957).

Sadler, J. & Walsh, S., *Flodden 1513*, Osprey Campaign Series 168 (Oxford, 2006).

Sadler, S. & Serdiville, R., *The Battle of Flodden 1513* (Stroud, 2013).

Scott, J, *The Men of Warre: The Clothes, Weapons and Accoutrements of the Scots at War, 1460–1600*, Retinue to Regiment Series No. 16 (Helion & Co., Warwick, 2023 (1)).

Scott, J, '"When Barwycke was Wonne": Richard of Gloucester in Scotland', *Battlefield, The Magazine of the Battlefields Trust*, Vol 28, Issue 1 (Autumn 2023 (2)).

Sherley-Price, L. (trans.), *Bede: A History of the English Church and People* (Harmondsworth, 1955).

Spiers, E., Crang, J. & Strickland, M. (eds), *A Military History of Scotland* (Edinburgh, 2012).

Stenton, F., *Anglo-Saxon England*, 3rd Edition (Oxford, 1968).

Stow, G.B. (ed.), *Historia Vitae et Regni Ricardi Secundo* (Philadelphia, 1977).

Stretton, M., *Piercing Plate Armour With Arrows: Empirical Testing at Bosworth Battlefield Centre* (Konig Books UK, 2018).

Strickland, M. & Hardy, R., *The Great Warbow* (Stroud, 2005).

Swanton, M. (ed.), *The Anglo-Saxon Chronicles* (London, 2000).

Taylor, S., Watt, D. & Scott, B., *Scotichronicon* (Aberdeen, 1987–98).

Tristram, K., *The Story of Holy Island* (Norwich, 2009).

Tyson, C., 'The Battle of Otterburn: When and Where was it Fought?' in Goodman & Took (eds) (1992).

Underwood, R., *Anglo-Saxon Weapons and Warfare* (Stroud, Gloucestershire, 1999).

Wood, M., *Domesday: A Search for the Roots of England* (London, 1986).

Woolf, A., *From Pictland to Alba 789–1070* (Edinburgh, 2007).

Woosnam-Savage, R., *Arms and Armour of Late Medieval Europe*, Royal Armouries Arms & Armour Series (Leeds, 2017).

Younger, P., 'Crouching Enemy, Hidden Ally: The Decisive Role of Groundwater Discharge Features in Two Major British Battles, Flodden 1513 and Prestonpans 1745', in Rose, E. & Mather, J. (eds), *Military Aspects of Hydrogeology* (Geological Society, London, 2012).

See also English Heritage Battlefield reports at historicengland.org.uk, cited in relevant chapters.

Index